MEAT ON THE GRILL

NEW RECIPES FOR BEEF, LAMB, PORK AND OTHER MEATS

BY
DAVID BARICH AND THOMAS INGALLS

PHOTOGRAPHY BY
DENNIS BETTENCOURT

FOOD STYLING BY
ROBERT BURNS

 HarperPerennial
A Division of HarperCollins*Publishers*

We would like to thank the following retailers, galleries, and individuals, all of whom helped in many ways to make this book look the way it does.

Filamento; Shiki, Inc.; Zosaku; Primavera; The Gardener; Dandelion; Cottonwood; ACCI Gallery; Gumps; Kembali; Diane Blacker Porcelain; Kitty Purrington; Heath Ceramics, Inc.; Steven Friedland; Leo Hobaica; Joan Platt; Addie Jenkins; Eric Norstad Pottery; Spangler Pottery; Gary Noffke; Sandra Simon; Kathleen Rumbager; Marni Turkel; Mark Prieto; Eve Lurie; Kurt McVey; Frank Fabens; John Shimizu; Peter & Frank Flannery; Silio Antonelli; Theresa Meyer; Kelly White; Paul Lagatutta; John Whitehill; Jan & Toni Heyneker; Summer House Mill Valley; Sylvan-Marshall; Allyson Anthony; Vera Burns; Garth Phillips; Kit Morris; Kepa Askansy; Craig Maxwell; Barb Schultheis.

A special note of thanks to Carolyn Miller for all her ideas, help, and suggestions.

Dedicated to John Barich (in sombrero), who was famous among family and friends for grilling lamb over an open fire.

For information, write:
HarperCollins Publishers, Inc.
10 East 53rd Street
New York, NY 10022

Printed in Hong Kong.

FIRST EDITION

Produced by David Barich.
Book and Cover Design: Ingalls + Associates
Designers: Tom Ingalls, Tracy Dean,
  Margot Scaccabarrozzi
Photography: Dennis Bettencourt
Photographer's Assistant: Jean Lannen
Prop Stylist: Abby Minot

**Library of Congress Cataloging-
in-Publication Data**

Barich, David.
     Meat on the grill : new recipes for beef, lamb, pork, and other meats / by David Barich & Thomas Ingalls ; photography by Dennis Bettencourt ; food styling by Robert Burns. — 1st ed.
          p.   cm.
     Includes bibliographical references and index.
     ISBN 0-06-096912-1 (paper).
     1. Barbecue cookery.   2. Cookery (Meat)   I. Ingalls, Thomas.   II. Title.
TX840.B3B355   1992
641.5'784—dc20   92-53399
                                                   CIP

93 94 95 96 10 9 8 7 6 5 4 3 2 1

The first epigraph is reprinted from *The Pursuit of Pleasure* by Lionel Tiger, published by Little, Brown and Company (Boston, 1992).

We can be certain that smoking food or cooking it over an open fire was a bedrock experience of evolving human beings during the first quarter of a million years in which we had some control over the use of fire. It takes no gymnastics of the imagination to decide that contemporary affection for smoky tastes recalls Sunday dinner at the hearth of the first family's cave.

Lionel Tiger
The Pursuit of Pleasure

"OFather, the pig, the pig, do come and taste how nice the burnt pig eats."

Charles Lamb
"A Dissertation Upon Roast Pig"

Contents

Introduction

It's not hard to believe that our love of grilled food is both deep and ancient. Grilling is one of those pleasures that are always described as *primordial,* or going back to the beginning of human life. Writers who try to define just why this form of cooking is so appealing usually find it to be an impossible task. The appeal of the grill has something to do with an open fire, with cooking directly over burning coals. It has something to do with the appearance of grilled foods: the marks of the grill grids, the crisp, slightly charred exterior of meat, and the juicy interior flesh. It has something to do with the fragrance of charcoal and cooking food, with being outside and cooking under the open sky, and with cooking with or for others—and all of it together seems to signify the beginning of cuisine, of civilization and the pleasures of the table. Even those who prefer to limit their consumption of red meat respond to the sensual appeal of the grill, for grilling is quite simply the most satisfying of all cooking methods for certain cuts of beef, pork, veal, and lamb.

There is no way of knowing how humans first learned that cooked meat was an entirely different order of food from raw, but Charles Lamb's little fable seems as good a story as any. In "A Dissertation Upon Roast Pig," he tells us that the first cooked meat was the result of a careless boy's accidentally burning down his family's hut with a litter of pigs inside. Soon houses all over the village were going up in smoke:

> The thing took wing, and now there was nothing to be seen but fires in every direction. Fuel and pigs grew enormously dear all over the district. The insurance-offices one and all shut up shop. People built slighter and slighter every day, until it was feared that the very science of architecture would in no long time be lost to the world. Thus this custom of firing houses continued, till in process of time, says my manuscript, a sage arose, like our Locke, who made a discovery, that the flesh of swine, or indeed of any other animal, might be cooked (*burnt,*

as they called it) without the necessity of consuming a whole house to dress it. Then first began the rude form of a gridiron.

Lamb's chronology of cooking techniques seems a little off, however. We can assume that meat first was cooked directly in the fire, then perhaps on coals or hot rocks in pits. Later came various methods devised to control the temperature of the fire and to prevent it from burning the food: suspending it from poles, attaching it to planks, piercing it on spits. What we think of as grilling couldn't technically begin until the Iron Age, when metal cooking racks eventually would be forged. Yet the Stone Age Indians of the Caribbean didn't wait on technology; they created woven green-wood grates to suspend foods over an open fire. The Indian word for these grates entered the Spanish language as *barbacoa.*

Grilling is thus an old and extremely simple method of cooking. Knowledge of the variables that affect cooking times and an attention to detail are its two great secrets. There are no tricky methods of preparation or cooking techniques. If you choose good meats, cook them to the proper doneness, and combine them with interesting marinades, sauces, and side dishes, you have guaranteed yourself a meal that will be uniquely satisfying for both you and your guests.

In *Meat on the Grill* we've chosen the cuts of meat that work best on the grill, and have given you specific cooking times and detailed turning and basting instructions for grilling them. Each of the twenty-five recipes includes a marinade and/or sauce or other embellishment, combined with suggested accompaniments to make great dinners for entertaining or for family. We've included old favorites, revised versions of standard recipes, and some of the newest ways to use both familiar and unusual foods. We hope you'll feel free to substitute side dishes and embellishments from other menus, or to come up with your own ways to glorify your perfectly grilled meat. We wish you happy grilling.

CHAPTER 1

GRILL BASICS: EQUIPMENT AND FIRE

GRILL BASICS: EQUIPMENT AND FIRE

Grilling can be made as simple or complex as you like, from an oven rack resting on a circle of stones around a wood fire to the latest in gas grills. All the recipes for this book were tested using a kettle grill, but they may be cooked on any of the grills discussed below. Two key elements in good grilling are gauging and manipulating the heat level of the fire and judging doneness, although on a gas grill, the first element is not a consideration, as the heat level is controlled automatically. Because so many variables affect the heat of a charcoal or wood fire, including wind and air temperature, it's important to learn to judge how hot the fire is burning. Depending on the kind of grill, there are various ways of altering the level of heat, such as opening and closing the grill vents, raising and lowering the cooking rack, adjusting the amount of fuel, adding or removing the hood, and checking the built-in temperature gauge. The basic information in this chapter will enable you to cook well on any grill in almost any weather.

CHARCOAL GRILLS

Kettle Grills: America's favorite, the kettle grill with its dome-shaped hood has the virtues of simplicity, affordability, and good design. It does have two drawbacks: First, the cooking rack is not adjustable, so the heat level must be manipulated by opening or closing the vents, adding or removing the hood, and moving the coals or the food. Second, it's hard to maintain a low fire for a long period of time in a kettle grill; for the long cooking of foods at low heat, the kamado works better. The kettle grill is constantly being improved and is available in different colors and in different sizes, from one small enough to carry on a picnic to the newest deluxe version, a kettle grill embedded in a steel cart (see "Console Grills," below). Good new features of kettle grills include enclosed ash catchers, which eliminate the mess of blowing ashes; tool hooks and a hood holder; a built-in temperature gauge; and charcoal baskets to hold coals for indirect grilling.

Console Grills: Larger, more expensive, and more elaborate than simple kettle grills, these rectangular grills may use either charcoal or gas and can be wheeled from place to place. The cooking rack is banked by work surfaces, some with inset cutting boards, so the problem of where to put food, dishes, and utensils is solved. A variety of attachments, an interior thermometer, a hood, and sometimes even a second rack unit make cooking on these grills almost as convenient as cooking on a traditional range in your own kitchen.

New grill models are blurring the line between kettle and console, and even between charcoal and gas: Some kettle grills are fueled by gas, and the newest console charcoal grill combines a kettle grill and a sturdy cart with a stainless steel work surface, a storage bin for charcoal, and an automatic gas starter. Because liquid propane gas burns cleaner than newspaper and kindling, this ignition system is an improvement over the charcoal chimney. This grill may be the best of both worlds—all the flavor and romance of charcoal, with the convenience and reliability of gas.

Kamados: The Japanese word *kamado* means variously "oven," "cooker," "smoker," "stove," or "fireplace," and the kamado is a versatile cooking implement indeed. This distinctive-looking ceramic cooker is made in Japan and is available in several different sizes and colors. The largest kamado will accommodate a 20-pound turkey. Although it is more expensive and much heavier than a kettle grill, it is also extremely durable and safe; it can even be installed for indoor cooking. The kamado is definitely the next step up for the grilling enthusiast. It has a removable interior ceramic ring that radiates heat evenly throughout the cooker, giving it the capabilities of a convection oven and making it an excellent choice for large pieces of food such as roasts and whole chickens and turkeys, and any other food that needs long cooking. Because of its double-walled construction, it retains and circulates heat from a low fire, thus allowing food to stay juicy inside.

Although the cooking rack is fixed some distance from the coals, the thick walls and the shape of the kamado enable it to function as a grill oven, much like the *tandoor* of India. The kamado also can be used as a smoke oven by adding wood chips to the charcoal: An optional removable top piece has adjustable vents with which to regulate the amount of smoke inside the kamado.

Because of its insulating construction, the kamado needs a minimum of charcoal, and about 80 percent of the charcoal can be used a second time. It gets hotter than other kinds of grills do (up to 500°F) and stays hotter longer, so it even can be used to bake bread. The kamado rests in a wheeled metal basket and thus is mobile.

Gas Grills

We are committed to charcoal grills; it seems to us that the flavor of charcoal is the essence of grilling, and we can't quite imagine enjoying this kind of cooking without it. Many people prefer gas grills, however, for their convenience and efficiency. Gas grills light instantly with the touch of a button, and they heat much faster than charcoal. Gas also burns more cleanly than charcoal. Like the kamado, gas grills work better than kettle or console grills for long, slow cooking, as the temperature is maintained automatically.

Needless to say, when you give up the taste of charcoal smoke, you also give up the problems of lighting and storing charcoal, as well as of cleaning up the ashes it leaves behind. The best use of gas grills may be in cooking for large groups of people—the reliability of a quickly lighted, even, and adjustable heat source can't be denied, and the easy cleanup afterwards is a bonus. Like charcoal grills, gas grills are constantly being refined and improved. Here are some things to look for if you're planning to buy a gas grill, and some things to be aware of when using one.

Buying a Gas Grill

Gas grills are still expensive when compared to charcoal grills, even though the more elaborate console charcoal grills are approaching some gas grills in price. Gas is cheaper to burn than charcoal: A 5-gallon tank of liquid propane gas will last for more than 24 hours of cooking and costs about $8. To find a licensed propane dealer to fill your fuel tank, look in the Yellow Pages under Gas, Propane.

Stationary gas grills are hooked up to a natural-gas line and usually consist only of a cooking rack and a fuel box on a pedestal. Portable gas grills use refillable canisters of either liquid propane or natural gas. They range from very small grills to carry on a picnic, to large consoles with all the conveniences of a large cooking surface, shelf space, a warming rack, a built-in timer, a fuel gauge, a window in the hood, a hood-mounted thermometer, and a dual-control burner.

The burners on gas grills are individually controlled and can be set to precise cooking temperatures. They are positioned under a bed of lava rocks (a grid covered with volcanic pumice), charcoal-like briquettes, clay pyramids, metal plates, or bars; this material radiates the heat of the burner to the food. One model features porcelain-coated steel triangles that channel fat to a drip pan, an arrangement that minimizes flare-ups.

The cooking rack may consist of either thin rods or wider bars; the bars act like a grill grid or basket and make it easier to cook fish fillets, hamburgers, and small pieces of food such as sliced vegetables. Most racks are made of porcelain-coated steel, though one model has a cast-iron rack.

Although the taste of charcoal is sacrificed for the convenience of cooking with gas, food acquires a smoky taste from the smoke created by the fat and juices dripping onto the lava rocks or other heat-distributing material. Some gas grills have smokers: built-in metal compartments to hold wood chips, which add their smoky taste to the grilled foods. A smoker is not absolutely necessary, but it does simplify the process of adding aromatic smoke to your grilling. Alternately, you can add smoking woods to any gas grill by using a disposable aluminum pie pan or by fashioning a container from aluminum foil. Poke holes in the bottom of the pan or the container to let the smoke escape, place the soaked wood chips inside, and set the pan or container directly on the lava rocks before lighting the grill.

All gas grills have hoods, and most of them have built-in or optional rotisserie attachments to hold several whole chickens or roasts, a great convenience when cooking for a large group. Another useful feature is a built-in side burner (like a burner on a gas stove), with its own heat control, to use for making sauces. Some gas grills have shelves that fold down for storage; others have removable shelves.

Other important features of gas grills are heavy, durable materials and strong construction. If you have a small backyard, make sure the gas grill you buy requires little clearance. Check the ignition button to make sure the gas jets light easily. Temperature controls should be either shielded or at a distance from the heat. A grill with a wooden handle on each side of the hood is a little safer than one with a handle on the front of the hood. Look for locking casters; these are especially helpful on large, heavy grills, because they allow the grill to be moved without being lifted on one side.

Ask whether the fuel tank is easy to change; a loaded fuel tank weighs almost 40 pounds, and the design of some grills makes it hard to attach. After attaching the tank to the grill, you will need to attach the pressure regulator to the tank; this device is connected to the gas line. On most grills this is done using a wrench, but a few grills have a snap-on fitting and the task may be accomplished without tools. Also, you should check to see how much of the grill you choose is delivered pre-assembled, and how difficult the assembly will be. Unless you are a mechanical whiz, it may be better to pay to have your grill delivered already assembled.

Make sure your grill preheats quickly; the average heating time is around 10 minutes, but some grills take much longer and may not be much faster than charcoal grills. The maximum heat output of a grill is measured in British thermal units, or Btu's; each unit is 1,000 per hour. A high Btu rating is not essential for good grilling, but it does mean that the grill should preheat faster.

Gas grills are especially easy to keep clean. Not only do you not have to worry about handling charcoal and cleaning up its ashes, but also most grills are largely self-cleaning if you use the following method: Turn the burners to high, close the lid, and leave the heat on for 15 minutes (lava rocks and briquettes should be turned upside down first). One grill has a removable bottom that can be washed in a sink.

Cooking with Gas

It's important to follow safety guidelines when cooking with gas. Most gas grills have an igniter that lights the gas with a spark. If the igniter is defective or is clogged with grease or dirt, it may not light at all, causing a gas buildup that can flare dangerously. First read the manufacturer's instructions carefully, then proceed using these basic rules:

• The hood must be completely opened before the grill is ignited.

• After opening the gas tank valve, turn the right side of the burner (if your grill has a burner with independent temperature controls) to High or Preheat.

• Avert your face and push the ignition button. If the burner does not light within 5 seconds, shut off the gas. Wait at least 5 minutes before attempting to relight the grill. Use a long fireplace match to light the burner, then have the igniter adjusted or replaced.

• After the right side of the burner is lighted, turn on the second side and it will be ignited by the first.

• Preheat the grill until the grids reach a temperature of 600°F. The preheating time on different grills may vary from as little as 4 minutes to more than 20 minutes.

• Sear food on high heat, then turn the temperature to medium for smaller pieces of food, and low for larger pieces.

• Keep the cooking rack clean by scrubbing it with a wire brush immediately after cooking; racks are much easier to clean when warm.

• *Never spray water on a gas grill.* Any flare-ups should be handled by closing the hood and turning down the heat. Using a drip pan and trimming the food of fat will help limit flare-ups, especially if the fuel bed is made of lava rocks, as grease tends to pool on this type of surface.

• Oil the cooking rack after it has been heated, using a long-handled brush, a piece of fat held in long-handled tongs, or a vegetable-oil spray.

• Make sure your grill is out in the open air, away from any surfaces, including the eaves of a roof, that might catch fire.

• When transporting a filled fuel tank in your car, place it so that it cannot move. Plug the opening of the hose fitting, and keep your car windows open.

• Filled fuel tanks should never be stored inside a house.

• Clean the burner system periodically; clogged tubes are dangerous. See the manufacturer's instructions for this task.

- Do not cook on any grill while wearing loose clothing such as a long shirt, loose sleeves, or long scarves.

OTHER GRILLS

A wide variety of other kinds of grills exists, from the hibachi and the brick backyard barbecue to the built-in kitchen or fireplace grill. **Stove-top grills** and free-standing **electric grills** are popular for indoor cooking because they are so easy to use. Most of these open grills are smokeless, and, like an oven broiler, they give a crisp, seared exterior to food without added oils. Because the flavor of smoke and charcoal will be missing, it's a good idea to use flavored bastes and marinades. Since they do not have a hood, these grills are limited to small pieces of food that cook quickly, such as sliced vegetables, boneless chicken breasts, and hamburgers.

Charcoal-Water Smokers: These tall, cylindrical smokers concentrate the smoke from charcoal and smoking woods in their narrow confines. Built in layers, beginning with a fuel grate and a water pan topped by one or more cooking racks, they have adjustable vents to control the level of smoke. People who love smoked foods swear by these grills, which produce moist foods strongly flavored with wood smoke. Any of the recipes in this book that use smoking woods can be adapted to a charcoal-water smoker by following the manufacturer's instructions. You also can add moisture and flavor to indirectly cooked food in any covered grill by adding water or marinade to a drip pan (see "Indirect Grilling," page 18).

CHARCOAL AND WOOD

Mesquite Charcoal: Mesquite cookery is not just a fad: This lump charcoal is popular because is an excellent fuel. Mesquite charcoal burns faster and cleaner than briquettes and hotter than either briquettes or other hardwood charcoal. Mesquite lends grilled foods a distinctive, subtle fragrance as well. When first lighted, mesquite sends off an alarming number of sparks, so it's important to stand away from the fire and make sure that your grill is not near any flammable material. You should break up large pieces of mesquite with a hammer, but remember that it catches fire and burns quickly, so don't make the pieces too small. Unburned lumps of mesquite can be relighted and used a second time.

Because mesquite burns at such a high temperature—up to 1,000°F—the initial stages of a red-hot fire may be too hot for searing or fast grilling.

The main disadvantage of mesquite and other hardwood charcoals is that they can be hard to find in many parts of the country. If you are dedicated to good grilling, you may want to order enough mesquite and/or other hardwood charcoal by telephone or mail to last you through the year. Thanks to 800 numbers, this is simple; see Equipment and Food Sources on page 88 for the addresses and telephone numbers of hardwood charcoal suppliers.

Hardwood Charcoal: Other woods besides mesquite, such as oak and ash, are made into lump charcoal. Like mesquite, they burn cleanly, with a minimum of ash. They also burn hotter than briquettes, but at their hottest they burn at around 800°F—not quite as hot as mesquite. Also like mesquite, they add their particular subtle fragrance to food, and leftover lumps can be re-lighted and used again.

Wood: Wood takes longer to reach the grilling stage of coal-readiness (about 1 hour), and it has a higher ash content than does lump charcoal. A combination of half hardwood charcoal and half wood will add the fragrance of wood smoke to your food. Make sure that the wood you use is whole, untreated hardwood, not softwood or any kind of processed wood, including lumber, that might contain chemicals.

Briquettes: Avoid cooking with briquettes if at all possible. Although they are cheaper in purchase price, they add chemical off tastes to your food and polluting gases to our air. Because they are made with fillers and binders, they have a higher ash content than do lump charcoals, so you will need to use more briquettes for any given grilling session. Briquettes also burn cooler than lump charcoal does, around 600°F, so they are not as effective for searing and open grilling.

PREPARING THE FIRE

Laying the Charcoal: For hardwood charcoal, spread a layer of large chunks over an area slightly larger than the area the food will cover on the cooking rack. For briquettes, spread a layer two-briquettes deep. *Please note:* If the recipe calls for more than 20 minutes of grilling, start with a larger quantity of charcoal, about half again as much, to allow for the longer cooking time. This is important to keep your fire from slowing down or dying, which means you will have to move the coals closer together, or add new coals and wait for the fire to heat up again before you can resume cooking.

Lighting the Charcoal: Try not to use liquid charcoal starter. Not only does it impart its chemical taste to food, it is damaging to the environment. And it's really not necessary—electric starters, kindling, or charcoal chimneys are just as fast, and all of these methods are safer, as well.

The simplest method of lighting charcoal is to use hardwood **kindling** with a wad or two of newspaper under it. Place the charcoal over the kindling, open the bottom vents of the grill, and light the newspaper (leave some air space between the briquettes and the kindling).

If you have an electric outlet near your grill, an **electric starter** may be your best choice, although it does take slightly longer to get a charcoal fire started. Place the starter under the coals and then plug it in. Remove the starter as soon as the first coals are lighted—this usually takes 10 minutes or so.

What started out as a large coffee can with holes punched in the sides (with a beer-can opener) for ventilation is now sold as a tall black metal cylinder with a handle, and is the most popular alternative to liquid starter. Because the **charcoal chimney** confines the charcoal in a smaller air space, kindling is not needed; instead, 1 or 2 sheets of crumpled newspaper are placed in the bottom section of the chimney, and medium-sized chunks of lump charcoal are piled in the top. The cooking rack is removed, the bottom grill vents are opened, and the chimney is placed on the fuel grate. Now the newspaper is lighted, and the chimney sits until the top layer of coals are lighted but not flaming. At this point, the lighted coals are dumped onto the fuel grate and unlighted coals are placed on top.

This inexpensive device will eventually pay for itself because of the money you will save by not purchasing liquid starter. It's also simpler, cleaner, and safer to use, and it's even more reliable.

Now available in natural foods stores and some supermarkets, **wax fire starters** have no additives. They are excellent for camping and picnics, when you might not want to cart along the charcoal chimney.

PREPARING THE COOKING RACK

Make sure the cooking rack is clean every time you grill. The best way to do this is to clean the rack with a wire grill brush immediately after each use—it's much easier to clean the rack when it's warm and food hasn't had too much of a chance to cook onto the metal.

After the coals have been lighted, put the cooking rack in place over the coals so that the rack will be hot when food is placed on it—this will help the food to cook evenly.

If the cooking rack has been kept clean it's not usually necessary to oil it before cooking, unless you are grilling delicate fish or food that has a fragile coating. If you didn't clean the rack after your last grilled meal, you may have to use steel wool to do so; in this case, oil the rack after it has heated, using a long-handled brush, a piece of fat held in long-handled tongs, or a vegetable-oil spray.

KNOW YOUR FIRE

The key to good grilling is knowing your fire. A slew of variables, including the temperature of the air and the amount of wind, can affect a fire's heat level and the rate at which it burns. Learning to gauge the heat of the fire lets you know when to start grilling and when to adjust the heat level for fast- or slow-burning fires, and consequently how to adjust cooking times. It's all a matter of attention to detail, plus a little experience.

Plan on allowing 45 minutes to elapse from the time you light the charcoal until you are ready to grill; hardwood requires about 1 hour. There are three distinct stages of heat for a charcoal or wood fire:

Hot: At this level, glowing red coals will be covered lightly with white ashes. If you hold your hand about 6 inches from the cooking rack at this stage, you will have to move it away after 3 or 4 seconds. This is the stage for searing and for quick grilling. Be sure not to put food on the grill if the fire is any hotter than this.

Medium-hot: When the fire is medium-hot, you will barely be able to see the red glow of the coals through a thicker layer of ashes, and you will be able to keep your hand 6 inches from the cooking rack for 5 to 7 seconds. This is the best stage for covered grilling.

Low: At this stage, the coals are completely gray, with no visible red glow. A low fire is best for the long, slow cooking of foods in a covered grill.

REGULATING THE FIRE

If the fire is burning too slowly or too fast for your purposes, three simple methods will allow you to regulate the heat:

Adjusting the Vents: Open the bottom and top vents of the grill to let more air into the grill and make the fire burn hotter. Partially close the vents to cool down the fire. (The bottom vent of a kettle grill also serves as an outlet for ashes from the bottom of the fuel grate.)

Adjusting the Coals: Move the coals apart to lower the heat of the fire, and move them closer together to intensify the heat.

Knocking Off the Ashes: If the coals have built up a thick layer of ashes and you want the fire to burn a little hotter, simply shake the grill or tap the coals with a grill utensil to remove the ashes.

If the fire is ready but you're not, put the cover on the grill with the vents partially closed; this will slow the fire until you're ready to grill.

COVERED GRILLING

Most of our recipes specify searing or browning meat over hot coals on an open grill, then covering the grill to finish cooking. Open grilling without a cover is best reserved for quick-cooking foods such as sausages, hamburgers, and sliced vegetables. Covering the grill lowers the heat of the fire and helps ensure that the meat will be juicy, not dried out. Unless you are cooking a large roast or adding smoking woods or other flavor enhancers to the coals, keep the upper vents on the grill cover open. You also may cover the grill and partially close the upper vents if you are trying to lower the heat of the fire before adding food to the cooking rack (see "Regulating the Fire," above).

INDIRECT GRILLING

"Indirect grilling" simply means that the food is not directly over the coals as it cooks in a covered grill. This technique makes your grill, in essence, a grill roaster, and should be be used for large pieces of food, such as roasts, that need a longer time to cook, as well as for fatty meats. In many cases, such as for smaller roasts, the meat can simply be moved to the side of the grill where the heat is less intense. For larger pieces of meat and fatty meats, you will want to move the coals to either side of the fuel grate and position the meat over a drip pan placed in the center of the grate.

Our favorite method of indirect grilling uses charcoal baskets, two curved metal charcoal containers that fit against the sides of kettle grills and are included with one deluxe model. These baskets cannot be purchased separately, but charcoal rails that serve the same function may be. These inexpensive metal rails are designed to fit on either side of a drip pan, although they may be used without one. They keep the coals stacked up, maintaining the heat level needed to keep the coals from going out. With baskets or rails, use about half again as many coals as you would use for direct cooking. Light a charcoal chimney filled with coals and, when they are fully lighted, divide them between the baskets or rails, then place unlighted coals on top.

An alternate method is simply to push fully lighted coals to either side of the grill; in this case, use about twice as many coals as you would for direct grilling, to keep the fire from dying. We prefer to make two banks of coals rather than pushing the coals into a circle, as the coals are more likely to die out in that formation.

Place an aluminum pie pan or rectangular baking pan in the center of the fuel grate and position the roast on the cooking rack over it. This will help keep the grill clean and eliminate flare-ups. The heat from the indirect fire will cook the roast slowly and evenly. Check the coals periodically to make sure the heat stays high, and stir, shake, or move the coals closer together if the fire has decreased.

To add both moisture and flavor to the cooking food, you can simulate a water-smoker by placing water in the drip pan. Add wine or vinegar, orange or lemon peels, or fresh or dried herbs to the water to flavor the smoke. Check the drip pan periodically to see if you need to add more liquid. This technique has the advantages of saving the cooking juices and of reducing the liquid in the drip pan to be used as a concentrated sauce for the food being grilled.

Vegetables can be cooked in the drip pan while a roast is cooking. Try placing vegetables that would normally be braised or baked, such as peeled whole or halved root vegetables, artichokes, or sliced or halved winter squash, in an inch or so of water or broth in the drip pan. The juices from the grilling roast will add their savory tastes to the vegetables. If the meat will cook less than half an hour, parboil the vegetables first.

FLARE-UPS

If you are careful not to use too hot a fire, you will avoid most flare-ups. If flare-ups do occur, move the food to the side of the grill and wait until the fire has burned down. Partially closing the vents and covering the grill also will dampen most flames, as will moving the coals apart. If you are using a charcoal grill, always keep a spray bottle of water handy to douse any flare-ups that don't respond to these tactics (water should not be sprayed on gas grills).

COOKING TIMES AND JUDGING DONENESS

Although we have tested and timed all our recipes, our cooking times must be considered suggestions only, as so many variables affect how fast food cooks on the grill. (For a chart of suggested cooking times and doneness temperatures for specific meats, see Chapter 2, page 25.) The temperature of the food, the fire, and the air are important factors, as is the level of humidity and whether or not it's windy outside. On damp days, food will cook more slowly; wind will make a fire burn hotter. As mentioned earlier, hardwood charcoal, including mesquite, burns hotter than briquettes. All of our recipes specify that the meat should be at room temperature at the time it's put on the grill. This is one of the most important things you can do to ensure good grilling; it gives you more control over the length of cooking time, and will allow any food to cook more evenly.

Experience in grilling and attention to detail will help you learn how to judge the heat of a fire and when meat is perfectly cooked. An instant-read thermometer is the most reliable aid in judging doneness, and an in-grill thermometer will help you maintain the correct level of heat, as it allows you to tell at once whether the heat inside the grill is high, medium, or low. Touch and sight tests for judging doneness work better with poultry and fish than with meats, although you can get an idea of the doneness of steaks by pressing on the meat with a tool or a finger to gauge its resistance to touch: If the meat is soft, it will be rare; if slightly resistant, it will be medium; and if stiff, it will be well done. Other than the desired degree of brownness and charring and the internal temperature, the best test for doneness of meat is to remove the meat from the grill and cut into it with a sharp knife. Don't hesitate to use this test, especially if you do not have an instant-read thermometer; meat can overcook in matter of minutes.

REPLENISHING THE COALS

A charcoal fire will burn for about 1 hour before it needs new coals, so you may have to replenish the coals when cooking large pieces of meat, such as the crown roast on page 70, even if you used extra coals to start with. If you know you will need extra coals, you can save time by lighting coals in a charcoal chimney set on a fireproof surface about 10 minutes before you think you will need them; then you will be able to proceed with your cooking right after the fully lighted coals are added to the fire.

If you haven't used enough coals, and if shaking the coals or moving them together doesn't increase the heat of the fire, you will need to add new coals. New mesquite added to a low fire will be ready to cook over in 10 to 20 minutes; briquettes will take a little longer. Remove the food from the cooking rack before adding the new coals, and note the time so that you'll know how much longer you'll need to finish the cooking.

Adding Flavors to the Fire

Most of our recipes for grilled meat call for an initial searing on each side followed by covered grilling; we think this is the best way to keep meat juicy. Covered grilling also provides a fine opportunity for adding extra flavor to meat with the use of aromatic woods and herbs. Smoking woods are now available in bits, chips, and chunks. The most common woods are hickory and mesquite, but you also will find alder, olive wood, apple, and other fruit woods.

Wood bits are usually soaked in water, then sprinkled over the coals whenever you want to add a light touch of smoke to foods. Follow the directions on the packaging for preparing wood chips; usually these are soaked in water for about 30 minutes. Wood chunks will need to soak for about 1 hour. If you use your own smoking woods, be sure not to use treated lumber. Remember not to overdo on the quantity of wood chips or chunks—you don't want their smoky flavor to overpower the taste of the meat.

Other flavor enhancers for the grill are vine cuttings, fresh or dried herb sprigs and twigs, dried fennel branches, grapevine cuttings, bay leaves and branches, and citrus peels. Both fresh and dried citrus peels, like wood chips and chunks, should be soaked in water before being added to the fire; use them to complement meats that have a citrus marinade or sauce. Fresh or dried herbs should also be soaked and may be used to complement meats when the marinade, stuffing, or sauce uses the same herb or herbs. Dried fennel branches, the dried leaves and branches of bay trees (also known as laurel trees), and fresh or dried sprigs or branches of rosemary and thyme are among the best choices of herbal flavorings to add to your coals.

Storing Charcoal

If you plan to grill on a regular basis, we suggest buying several large bags of mesquite or other hardwood charcoal and dumping them all in a large plastic or metal trash can with a tight-fitting lid. Keep the can right next to your grill, where the charcoal will stay dry and available for use any time you get the urge to fire up the coals.

Cleaning the Grill

As we mentioned earlier, by far the best time to clean the cooking rack is immediately after use. A wire grill brush is indispensable for this task. Cleaning the cooking rack with a wire brush takes hardly any time when the rack is still warm. If you do have to resort to steel wool to clean a cold cooking rack, season it afterward by rubbing cooking oil on the grids.

Putting the Fire Out

If you have an open grill without a cover, you should pour a little water over the coals and check them later to make sure they have gone out. If you have a covered grill, just close all the vents and cover the grill. If you have used hardwood charcoal, you will usually be able to use the leftover coals the next time you cook; to light used coals, smother them with new, lighted coals from the charcoal chimney.

Tools for the Grill

Grilling tools make grilling much easier. The following is a list of the tools that we think are important; the ones marked with an asterisk are those we wouldn't want to be without.

★Charcoal chimney: Unless you have an electric starter or an always available stash of kindling, you should buy a charcoal chimney. You'll never have to deal with liquid starter again.

★Long-handled tongs: These metal tongs are spring-loaded, so you have more control. Look for the ones found in restaurant supply stores; they are more strongly built and are reasonably priced. This all-purpose utensil is best for picking up pieces of food; it can also be used to adjust coals, and its scalloped, spoonlike tips can be used for basting.

★Wire grill brush: This tool is the answer to the problem of how to keep the cooking rack clean, an essential step in good grilling. A clean cooking rack prevents foods from sticking to the grill and ensures that rancid or off flavors from previously cooked foods don't affect whatever you're currently grilling.

★Instant-read thermometer: A little more expensive than regular food thermometers, but worth it. In fact, we think the instant-read thermometer is one of the most important tools for good grilling. It takes the worry out of determining doneness and saves you both time and the disappointment of overcooked food. The instant-read thermometer immediately tells you the interior temperature of foods and thus gives you more control over the grilling process.

★Spray bottle: Keep a spray bottle filled with water on hand as a last resort in putting out flare-ups in charcoal grills, but *do not* spray water on a gas grill.

Grill mitts: You can use oven mitts for grilling, but extra-long heavy-duty grill mitts will give you much more protection against burns.

Bent-blade spatula: The turning surface of this spatula is set at an angle to the handle, which makes this tool much easier to use and gives you more control when turning food. It's especially good for turning such delicate foods as breaded chicken or fish fillets, and small pieces of food such as sliced vegetables. Choose the long-handled variety made for grilling.

Basting brush: Although a long-handled brush for basting is not essential (you can use a big spoon or the tip of your tongs), it is nice to have one.

Skewers: Soak wooden skewers in water for at least 15 minutes before using to keep them from burning up on the grill. Thread medium-sized pieces of food on two parallel wooden or metal skewers to prevent the food from turning.

★Timer: It's easy to lose track of time, especially when cooking for a group, as is often the case with grilling. Use a kitchen timer and reset it for each phase of the grilling process. Look for the type that clips onto your apron, so you'll be sure to hear it ring.

Grill thermometer: Designed to be kept inside a covered grill, this thermometer will give you more control over long-cooked foods such as large roasts.

Drip pans: Metal pie pans make good drip pans and can be easily cleaned and reused if they are soaked right after using.

★Nonaluminum marinade containers: When marinating foods, you can use almost anything except uncoated aluminum, which tends to give acidic marinating ingredients such as tomatoes, vinegar, wine, and citrus juice a metallic off taste. We prefer shallow oval baking dishes of either glass or ceramic for small pieces of meat, and large glass or ceramic bowls for roasts.

Grill basket: This hinged wire basket makes it easy to turn hamburgers and thin pieces of meat; it's also great for sliced vegetables and fruit, and fish fillets.

Grilling grid: Operating on the same principle as the grill basket, this perforated metal sheet sits on top of the cooking rack and is used to grill small pieces of food that would otherwise fall through the grids of the cooking rack. The foods must be turned, however, preferably with a bent-blade spatula, in order to grill the other side. A grilling grid is helpful for cooking hamburgers, fish, fruit, and vegetables. A piece of metal screening is a good substitute.

★Knives: Good knives are invaluable for any kind of cooking.

★Cutting board: For cutting up raw meats, it's best to have a plastic or acrylic cutting board that is kept solely for use with flesh foods. These inexpensive cutting boards will not harbor bacteria as do wooden cutting boards. Be sure to wash your cutting board with hot soapy water after each use; plastic or acrylic boards may be washed in a dishwasher.

Carving board: It's nice to have a separate carving board for meats, although you can use a clean plastic or acrylic cutting board. Wooden boards made especially for carving have grooves that will collect meat juices, which can then be added to a cooked sauce or passed in a pitcher to pour over the sliced meat.

Charcoal rails: These inexpensive metal rails shore up stacks of charcoal on either side of a grill and help to keep an indirect fire going. Because the coals are stacked, they burn more steadily and are not as likely to go out as coals placed in a circle or simply pushed to either side of the grill.

CHAPTER 2
GRILLING MEATS

GRILLING MEATS

Try to find the best meat possible when buying for the grill. If you are concerned about growth hormones and antibiotics in meat, look for naturally raised meats in natural foods stores, or ask your market about carrying them.

Doneness Temperatures for Meats

Beef, lamb, and venison:
Rare 140°F
Medium rare 150°F
Medium 160°F
Well done 170°F

Pork and veal: 150°F

Steaks and Chops

Although many people grill steaks and chops uncovered, we usually prefer to sear them for a few minutes on each side and then finish cooking them covered, as we think it makes for juicier and tastier meat. Make sure that steaks and chops are cut at least 1 inch thick, to keep them from overcooking—1½ inches is even better.

For each inch of thickness, cook steaks and chops for a total of about 6 minutes for rare, 8 minutes for medium rare, 10 minutes for medium, and 12 inches for well done.

Roasts

Cook roasts over indirect heat; for large roasts and all fatty roasts, use a drip pan to keep the grill clean and to prevent flare-ups. Boneless rolled beef, lamb, and venison roasts should be cooked for about 15 minutes per pound for rare, 17 minutes per pound for medium rare, 20 minutes per pound for medium, and 25 minutes per pound for well done. Pork and veal boneless rolled roasts should be cooked for 17 to 20 minutes per pound.

Ground Meats

Look for meat with a fair amount of fat for grilling; fat helps to keep ground meat juicy and adds to the flavor. We prefer ground chuck for hamburgers, as it has a little less fat than regular ground beef and a little more than ground sirloin. For a variety of grilled hamburgers, see page 54. We also like lamb burgers and molded shish kabobs of spiced lamb or pork. Remember not to pack ground meat together tightly; it should be molded just enough to hold together on the grill. A grilling grid or a grill basket is handy for grilling hamburgers.

Sausages

One of the easiest and best foods for grilling, especially now that so many kinds of sausages are available. We like to combine an assortment of several kinds of sausage, from classic German wursts and Italian sausages to newer varieties such as chicken and basil, chicken and apple, Thai-flavored chicken, smoked turkey, and various kinds of duck sausage. Look for low-sodium, non-nitrate fresh sausages and grill them within 24 hours of purchase; these sausages also can be frozen.

To grill sausages, prick each one in several places with a fork to keep it from bursting, and cook over medium-hot coals until lightly browned on all sides; then cover the grill to finish cooking, turning the sausages several times, for a total cooking time of 8 to 12 minutes, depending on the thickness of the sausages. The best test for doneness is to cut into one to make sure it is no longer pink inside.

A GLOSSARY OF MEATS FOR THE GRILL

BEEF

Beef is the favorite meat for grilling in this country, and the best cuts range from the simple hamburger to the luxurious whole tenderloin. Any naturally tender cut of beef that can be eaten rare or medium rare is good for the dry heat of the grill, but cuts for grilling can be found in each of the nine primal, or basic, cuts of beef. The two grades of beef preferred for grilling are Prime and Choice. Prime beef has more marbling, and this larger amount of fat makes it more tender and more tasty. It also makes it more expensive, and most Prime beef usually is reserved for restaurants. Choice beef is perfectly adequate for the grill, however, and its slightly lower fat content may be preferable to many.

The whole subject of meat cuts is a confusing one; the physical structure of a steer is complex, different butchers in different parts of the country have different names for the same cuts of meat, and the same muscle changes names depending on which section of the steer it is found in. A little understanding of anatomy goes a long way to clearing up the confusion, so we've given you a tour of the animal, discussing each primal cut beginning in the mid-section with the three most tender ones.

The central upper section of the steer includes the most tender meat. Three primal sections—the rib, the short loin, and the sirloin—contain two horizontal muscles that yield the most expensive and luxurious cuts of beef. These muscles are the tenderloin and the muscle variously known as the rib eye, the top loin, or the sirloin, depending on which primal section it is found in.

Rib

The rib section is found between the chuck and the short loin. The entire rib section, often called the prime rib, usually contains seven ribs; the rib "eye" is the tender heart of the rib roast, which runs horizontally through it. (The rib eye muscle, second in tenderness only to the tenderloin, is called the top loin when it is part of the short loin section, and is called the sirloin when it is part of the sirloin section.)

The small end of the rib section is the end closest to the short loin and is known as the **standing rib.** It contains a larger portion of the eye and is the most desirable for grilling. The small end of the standing rib section is the best portion. To grill, use indirect heat and a drip pan. Sear over a hot fire and cook, covered, for 10 to 15 minutes per pound, or to an internal temperature of 140°F for rare or 150°F for medium rare.

The rib section also is cut into **rib steaks,** which may be bone-in or boneless (the bones are sold as **beef back ribs** and may be grilled in the same way as spareribs; see page 77). The smaller steaks are nearer the short loin and will have more of the tender rib eye section; choose these for grilling. The rib eye itself is cut into boneless steaks and marketed as **rib eye steaks, Delmonico steaks,**

Spenser steaks, and **market steaks,** among others. All of these are excellent for grilling.

Short Loin

So called because it is the part of the loin section that is shorter, crosswise, than the sirloin, this part of the animal is the source of the most tender of all beef steaks. Three muscles are contained in the short loin, running horizontally through this cut of meat: the long, narrow tenderloin, which is tapered on one end; the long top loin (a continuation of the rib eye from the rib section), which curves partly around the tenderloin and is separated from it by the T-bone; and a little tail of meat that is part of the flank. Each section is separated from the others by a layer of fat or the T-bone. The narrower end of the short loin (and the tenderloin inside it) is closer to the front of the animal and next to the rib section; the wider end is closer to the hind section and is next to the sirloin.

Tenderloin: This is the most expensive of all beef cuts. Because the muscle is hidden inside the short loin, in the middle of the animal's back, it does very little work and thus is the most tender of all the muscles in its body. It is also relatively low in fat, having little marbling, and its flavor is delicate and should be complemented by lightly flavored sauces and side dishes. Because it is low in fat, this cut is often paired with sauces made with cream and butter, and served with side dishes that match the tenderloin in elegance, such as spring asparagus or wild mushrooms. The important things to remember are not to overwhelm the taste of the tenderloin with assertive flavors and not to overcook this high-ticket cut. Cooked properly, the tenderloin is one of the most elegant grill dishes you can serve, and thus it is perfect for special occasions. To grill, see the recipe on page 42.

Other names for the tenderloin are **beef fillet, filet mignon,** and **Chateaubriand,** although to the French, the filet mignon is the tapered end of the tenderloin, and Chateaubriand is a dish made from a section cut from the thick end. **Tournedos** are slices cut from the center of the tenderloin.

New York Strip Steak: Because this steak is cut from the narrow end of the short loin, it contains none of the tenderloin and consists only of the top-loin muscle. It is well marbled and flavorful, and it grills beautifully.

Make sure these steaks are cut thick, about 1½ inches. To grill, see our recipe on page 39. The New York strip is also known as a **club steak** and a **Kansas City strip steak.** Because the T-bone and the Porterhouse also contain the top loin muscle as well a part of the tenderloin, a New York strip can be cut from a portion of either of those steaks.

Porterhouse/T-bone Steak: These two large steaks are cut from the thicker part of the short loin and differ very little from each other. Each contains a portion of the top loin and varying amounts of the tenderloin and the flank (the last-named forming the "tail" of the steak). These steaks should be cut thick, like the New York strip. To grill, see the recipe on page 41. Because the top loin is included in this cut, you can use a more assertive marinade and/or sauce than when you are grilling only the tenderloin.

Sirloin: The word *sirloin* means "over the loin," and that is where this section of the animal is found, right between the short loin and the rump. It consists of the continuation of the tenderloin, the top sirloin (which is a continuation of the top loin found in the short loin section), and the bottom sirloin, which contains three different muscles. One of these is used to make **ground sirloin,** another becomes the **sirloin tip roast** or is cut into **kabobs,** and the third becomes the **culotte steak,** a well-flavored cut for grilling that is complemented by an assertive marinade. (Depending on how the animal is cut up, the sirloin tip roast may be cut from either the sirloin or the round.)

The meat from the sirloin is a little less tender than that of the short loin. There are various cuts of bone-in **sirloin steaks** that are fine for grilling (follow the directions for cooking Porterhouse steaks, page 41), but you might prefer boneless steaks cut from the top sirloin. Make sure they are cut thick for grilling, preferably 1½ inches. Cook these like the New York strip steak (see page 39).

Foreshank and Brisket

The brisket is the breast of the animal, and usually forms a primal cut with the foreshank, or front leg. The foreshank is used for stewing meat and ground beef, and the brisket usually is turned into corned beef, but it also can make a fine cut for grilling.

Brisket: Slightly chewy and very flavorful, the brisket is a good choice when grilling for large groups. The whole brisket is flat on one end and rounded on the other; when cut in half crosswise, the half with a flat end is called the "flat cut." This section has less fat and is a little more expensive than the rounded-end half, which is called the "point cut."

The brisket should be marinated for a relatively long time in a flavorful marinade and cooked covered over medium-hot to low heat. It can be eaten either rare or well done, and should be cut on the diagonal and served on country bread to make sandwiches, or as on page 47.

Chuck

This primal cut includes the front shoulder and neck; most of the meat from this section is used for pot roasts, Swiss steaks, and ground beef. We prefer **ground chuck** for grilled hamburgers, as the meat has just enough fat and flavor. One section of the chuck is often boned and rolled into a **boneless cross-rib roast,** which may be grill-roasted like any other boneless beef roast. The entire roast will weigh from 10 to 15 pounds. It is often cut into thirds (the tapered end is the most tender) or into steaks for the grill, which may be called **barbecue steaks** or some other generic term.

The **chuck short ribs** also come from this section. Although they are not as tender as short ribs from the plate section (see below), they also can be cut very thin across the bone ("flanken style") and grilled for Korean barbecued beef (see page 51).

Three other pieces of the chuck section can be grilled: a small muscle named the flatiron is usually sliced and marketed as **butter steaks;** another muscle sometimes called the **mock tender, chuck tender,** or **Jewish filet** may also be grilled whole or in slices. Because the blade end of the chuck is right next to the rib primal cut, the blade-cut chuck roast contains part of the rib "eye," and is often cut into **market** or **Spenser steaks** (see "Rib," above).

Round

The round is the hind leg of the animal, which may be cut into bone-in roasts, called **standing rump roasts** or **rolled boneless rump roasts.** Both of these are excellent grilled.

The round section also may be sliced into steaks (called full-cut round steaks), which contain some meat that is not tender enough for the grill, or divided into its four muscles: the tip, the top round, the eye of round, and the bottom round. Cuts from the tip and the top round are suitable for grilling.

The tip is marketed as a **sirloin tip** (it also runs horizontally through the sirloin, where it forms part of the bottom sirloin). It is sliced into **sirloin tip steaks** and may be called **London broil,** among other names; these are good choices for the grill. It is also cut in half and rolled into two **boneless sirloin tip roasts.** Each of these will weigh from 4 to 8 pounds and may be grilled.

The so-called **"first cut" of the top round** is also a good steak for grilling. This cut is closest to the sirloin and is thus more tender; it consists of an almost solid portion of meat without the striation of fat that shows the presence of another muscle. It is often marketed as **butterball steak** or **London Broil.**

The bottom round and eye of the round, although the latter is often sliced and marketed as **breakfast steaks,** generally are not tender enough for grilled steaks, although these cuts can be substituted for skirt steak and grilled for fajitas (see page 52).

Flank

The flank is the section of the belly of the steer nearest the hind legs. Much of this meat is tough and is used in ground beef, but the long muscle known as the **flank steak** is good for grilling when it is marinated for a fairly long time in an assertive marinade, grilled to medium rare, then thinly sliced on the diagonal (see the recipe on page 44). (The flank steak, like several other cuts of meat, is sometimes called "London broil," but as Merle Ellis points out in *Cutting Up in the Kitchen* (Chronicle Books, 1975), the flank steak is so misnamed because London Broil is the name of a recipe using flank steak.)

Plate

The plate is the section of the underside of the animal beneath the ribs. Most of it is used for ground beef, but it is also cut into **short ribs.** When these are cut into ¼-inch-thick slices across the bone, marinated in a spicy Asian-flavored sauce, and quickly grilled, they become Korean barbecued beef (see page 51).

Skirt Steak

Found inside the animal, the skirt is the diaphragm muscle. Although it is not naturally tender, it can be tenderized by being cut at an angle and marinated for a fairly long time. Quickly grilled and chopped into bits, this flavorful cut of beef becomes steak fajitas (see page 52).

LAMB

Lamb is probably the most commonly grilled meat in the world. It has a long history as a grilled food because it was and still is the staple meat for shepherds and small farmers in grazing lands in many countries. Classic recipes for lamb are an important part of the cuisines of the Mediterranean, the Levant, and India, among others. Unlike beef, virtually every cut of lamb is tender enough for grilling, and the assertive flavor of the meat is beautifully complemented by garlic, herbs, and the flavors of charcoal and aromatic wood smoke.

Loin

The loin section of the lamb corresponds to the short loin of beef. A full loin (which includes the backbone, or chine bone, and the loin meat on both sides of it), is usually tied and sold as a saddle of lamb or cut into chops called **double loin chops** or **English chops.** The bone-in saddle is fine for grilling, but the **boneless saddle of lamb** is a better choice because it cooks more evenly and is easier to carve and serve (see the recipe on page 58). If you grill lamb chops, make sure they are at least 1 to 1½ inches thick. Sear them for 1 minute on each side over hot coals, then cover and cook them for about 4 minutes on each side for medium rare.

The loin may be cut in half down the backbone and sold as two **loin roasts** or cut into **single lamb chops.** Both of these are fine for grilling. You also can make your own **boneless double-loin lamb roll** (which is essentially the same thing as a boneless saddle of lamb) by buying two lamb loin roasts, boning them out, and tying them together to form a roll. Like the boneless saddle of lamb, this is a versatile and elegant cut for grilling.

Sirloin

This section is usually sold as part of the leg, but it may also be sliced and sold as **leg chops** or **sirloin steaks.** Grill these as you would loin chops, or cut into meat for **kabobs.**

Grilling Meats **29**

Leg

The leg may be sold in its entirety ("full leg"), or cut into halves or a section called the "short leg" (three fourths of the full leg). Because the leg contains several bones and so is difficult to carve, the best section for grilling is the boned short leg. This can be rolled and tied, but we prefer the unrolled and flattened boneless leg, or **butterflied leg of lamb,** for grilling, as it cooks more quickly and more evenly. The different thicknesses of the various sections of a butterflied leg (the top leg muscle, the bottom leg muscle, and the "eye") mean that the meat will cook to different degrees of doneness, which is nice for serving a large group with varying preferences (see the recipe on page 61). The boned leg meat also may be cut into **kabobs** for grilling (see the recipe on page 62).

Rib Rack

The rib section of the lamb contains eight or nine ribs and is usually cut into single- or double-rib (double-cut) **lamb chops.** Either of these is fine for grilling, but the whole **rib rack** is easier to handle. One rack will feed 2 or 3 people. Make sure the butcher has cracked the chine bone between the ribs so you can carve the rack easily (see the recipe on page 56). You can make a **rolled rib roast** by boning two racks and tying them together (after removing the fell, which is the thin white membrane that covers the rack). Cut this roast into slices for **boneless rib chops,** if you like. Two or three rib racks can also cut tied together to form a **crown roast** after you have removed the chine bone; see the recipe for the crown roast of pork on page 70.

Shoulder

This primal cut contains the shoulder, the breast, and the shank (the latter is really the foreshank; the rear shank is sold as part of the leg). The shoulder may be boned and rolled to make a **boneless shoulder roast.** This relatively inexpensive cut can be substituted for the boneless saddle or boneless double rack and cooked in the same way. The shoulder is also excellent for cutting into meat for **kabobs.**

Breast of Lamb

Sometimes called **lamb spareribs,** this is the same section as the brisket in beef but is much more tender.

Grill the entire breast and cut it into rib sections to serve, or bone the breast, then roll it, tie it, and cut it into inch-thick slices. These pinwheel-shaped chops should be held together with toothpicks and grilled like lamb loin chops (see "Loin," above). Even **lamb shanks** can be grilled, covered, over a medium-hot to low fire; serve them over a bed of braised beans or sauerkraut.

PORK

Compared with beef and lamb, relatively few parts of the pig may be used for grilling. Yet those sections that are tender enough make wonderful grill meals, as the savory, rich flavor of pork is naturally complemented by the flavor of charcoal.

Loin

The pork loin is sold cut into three sections: the **blade- or rib-end pork loin,** the **center-cut pork loin,** and the **sirloin-end pork loin.** These correspond, respectively, to the rib section, the top loin, and the sirloin in beef. The center section has the largest portion of the tenderloin, as well as the least fat and bone, so it is also the most expensive. Any of the three sections may be cut into **pork chops** for the grill, or they may be boned, rolled, and grilled (see the recipe for **boneless pork loin** on page 69). Make sure chops are at least 1 inch thick for grilling (see the recipe for loin chops on page 64). Meat from any section of the loin may be cut into **kabobs** for grilling (see the recipe on page 73).

The ribs from the boned pork loin become **baby back ribs** (see the recipe on page 74). A butterflied blade-end pork roast becomes **country-style ribs;** these may be sliced into separate rib sections, but are easier to grill in their whole, butterflied state. Use any of the marinades for grilled pork in this book.

The **pork tenderloin** is the long muscle running through the heart of the loin section. As in beef, it is the most tender part of the pig, and its price reflects that. Also like the tenderloin of beef, it makes an elegant grill meal, easily cooked and perfect for pairing with a mild sauce (see the recipe on page 66).

Boston Shoulder

The upper shoulder section of the pig often is marketed as a **Boston shoulder** or **Boston butt.** It is cut into pork steaks or **kabobs,** and when boned makes an excellent roast for the grill.

Picnic Shoulder

The foreleg and lower shoulder of the pig, the picnic shoulder may be boned and rolled for a grill roast or cut into **kabobs.**

Ham

The hind legs of the pig may be sold as fresh hams but are usually turned into cured hams. Use a large quantity of coals to bake a **whole ham** in a kettle grill, or use a kamado or gas grill. Or grill thick slices of **ham steak** (at least 1 inch thick) until browned on each side and heated through, a total of about 10 minutes.

VEAL

Although veal is tender, it is also low in fat and thus fairly dry, so care must be taken when cooking it on the grill. If you are concerned about humane farming practices and about antibiotics in meat, try to find naturally raised veal rather than "Dutch-process" veal (see Equipment and Food Sources).

The loin of the calf is cut into **veal chops** or boned and rolled into **veal loin roasts.** Both are quite pricey, as are **veal cutlets** cut from the top loin. Both the leg and shoulder may be boned and rolled (the shoulder makes the least expensive roasts) and grilled as roasts or sliced into cutlets. Make sure that veal is at room temperature before grilling it.

Veal chops that are to be grilled should be cut 1 to 1½ inches thick. Brush them liberally with olive oil before grilling to keep them from drying out (see the recipe on page 81).

A boneless veal roast should have any added layer of fat removed. You will have to untie it (discard elastic strings). Unroll the roast and place pieces of the fat layer, pancetta, or blanched drained bacon inside to keep the meat moist while it is cooking, and retie the roast with cotton string. Be sure to brush it liberally with olive oil before grilling. The veal sirloin is usually boned and cut into thin **scallops,** which may be pounded flat to make **scaloppine** and rolled into stuffed veal rolls (see the recipe on page 83).

RABBIT

The lean white meat of domestic rabbit takes well to the grill. It should be marinated for a farily long time first (see the recipe on page 78). Fresh farm-raised rabbit is available in most butcher shops (you may have to order it; see also Equipment and Food Sources); one rabbit will weigh between 2 and 3 pounds.

VENISON

Fine-textured, low in fat, and dark in color, venison has a rich flavor that takes well to grilling. The **strip loin** may be grilled whole (see the recipe on page 86), and the **sirloin** may be cut into steaks or boned and rolled into roasts. The **boneless saddle of venison** and the **tenderloin** are other good cuts for the grill. Wild venison has a stronger taste than farm-raised animals. Farm-raised venison can be delivered overnight from several sources; New Zealand venison is considered to be especially good (see Equipment and Food Sources).

VARIETY MEATS

Calves' **liver,** veal and lamb **sweetbreads,** and veal or lamb **kidneys** all can be grilled. These delicate meats should be grilled quickly over an open medium-hot fire. The sweetbreads should be be cooked for 4 to 5 minutes on each side, the liver for 1 to 2 minutes on each side, and the kidneys for a total of 10 to 15 minutes while being turned frequently. For a special treat, cook any or all of these variety meats along with veal or pork chops and an assortment of sausages for a mixed grill; serve with several mustards and/or dipping sauces.

COOKING MEATS SAFELY

In the last few years, a rise in the number of outbreaks of salmonella has focused attention on the way in which meat and chicken are processed for the market. The consensus seems to be that the combination of mass production methods and a reduction in the number of federal food inspectors has increased the incidence of salmonella in all foods of animal origin, including meats, fish, poultry, eggs, and milk. Other worries have arisen about the safety of grilling meats because of the possibility that the carbonization of fat dripping on the coals may be dangerous. Because of these considerations, buy your meat from a reputable butcher and follow the following guidelines:

• Refrigerate uncooked meat as soon as possible after purchasing it. Don't leave meat or any other flesh foods in your car or unrefrigerated elsewhere for any length of time en route from market to home, especially when the weather is warm. If you know your trip from store to home will take over half an hour, bring along a cooler for storing milk, eggs, and flesh foods.

• Wash your hands with soap and hot water before handling raw meat.

• Use one cutting board, preferably an acrylic or plastic one, for flesh foods only; cut all other foods on a different board.

• After handling or cutting raw meat, wash your hands, utensils, and cutting board well in hot soapy water. Remember to wash sponges, dish towels, and dishcloths, too. Do not handle any other foods without first washing your hands.

• Don't let meat marinate at room temperature for more than 2 hours. To be ultra safe, marinate meat in the refrigerator.

• Any marinade that is to be used as a sauce after the meat is cooked should be boiled for several minutes before being served.

• Be sure to wash in hot, soapy water any dish in which uncooked meat was marinated and any vessel that was used to transfer the meat to the grill. Take care that no juices from uncooked meat come into contact with other foods.

• Current USDA guidelines recommend cooking all red meat to an internal temperature of 160°F, or to a medium degree of doneness, to be absolutely safe. Although there is a very minimal bacterial risk at temperatures below this, our suggested doneness temperature is 150°F, or medium rare, for all meats including pork, as we feel that higher temperatures dry out meat and tend to make it tough. Pork is safe from trichinosis at a temperature of 137°F.

• Don't allow meat to overcook; a heavily charred exterior is neither tasty nor good for you. Meat should be crisply browned, with just a light amount of charring, if you like.

• Don't cook large pieces of fatty meats such as pork roasts directly over the coals; use an indirect fire.

• All cooked meat should be refrigerated within 2 hours of being cooked.

PREPARING MEATS FOR THE GRILL

Follow the cleanliness guidelines above. Using a sharp slicing knife, remove all but about ¼ inch of exterior fat from the meat; pull the tissue-thin fell membrane off pieces of lamb. To bone your own roasts and cut chops for the grill, you will need a sharp boning knife, a butcher's steel, a cutting board, and a hacksaw. Most boning and slicing techniques are simple and obvious, but a book on cutting up meat will be helpful for some of the trickier preparations. Doing your own meat cutting can save you a considerable amount of money.

SECRETS OF THE GRILL: A LITTLE GUIDE TO GRILLING MEATS

• Observe the cleanliness guidelines in the section "Cooking Meats Safely," page 31.

• Use a marinade or a spice paste to help season the meat or, at the very least, rub the meat all over with oil before grilling. (When marinating, avoid uncoated aluminum or cast-iron containers, as the acidic content of the marinade can interact with the metal to create a metallic taste. Use glass, ceramic, enameled cast iron, coated aluminum, or stainless steel.)

• Make sure the meat is at room temperature before grilling. If it has been marinating in the refrigerator, remove it from the refrigerator for 30 minutes before cooking; roasts should sit at room temperature for about 45 minutes before being cooked.

• Keep the cooking rack clean with a wire grill brush; clean it after you finish cooking each time, while the rack is still warm.

• Most cuts of meat benefit from covered cooking after the initial searing or browning; exceptions are very thin slices of meat, and hamburgers.

• Use an indirect fire for roasts and other large pieces of meat, especially for fatty meats.

• *Pay attention to the cooking time!* It's hard to stress this one too much. It doesn't do much good to choose the best meat and to give it a loving marinade if you let it overcook and become dry. Because it's so easy to lose track of time, especially when cooking for a crowd, buy a kitchen timer that clips onto your apron.

• Although we've tried to give precise cooking times, these depend on so many variables that you should always check to make sure the meat is done to your liking. When in doubt, use an instant-read thermometer or cut into the meat.

• Allow large or thick pieces of meat to sit at room temperature for about 10 minutes after grilling; large roasts should sit for up to 20 minutes. This lets the juices settle inside the meat and keeps it juicy. You can cover the meat with aluminum foil to keep it warm if you like.

SPECIAL INGREDIENTS

Asian sesame oil: A little sesame oil goes a long way. The lightest touch of this condiment made from toasted sesame seeds is enough to give a smoky Far East taste to marinades.

Balsamic vinegar: This all-purpose wine vinegar derives its name not from anything to do with balsam wood, but because it was prized for many years in Italy as a medicinal balm, or *balsamo,* perhaps because of its mellow, comforting taste. (Vinegar traditionally has been used in many countries of the world as a medicine and as a poultice.) Produced in Modena, Italy, balsamic vinegar has a deeply sweet and rich flavor, the result of long aging in wood casks. Use this versatile ingredient in any number of salad dressings, in simple vinaigrettes, as a flavor enhancer for strawberries and other fruits, and as an inspired addition to marinades for vegetables, birds, and other foods to be grilled. (To make a simple marinade for grilled vegetables, combine balsamic vinegar with extra-virgin olive oil and salt and pepper to taste; add fresh herbs if you like.)

Broth: Short of making your own stock at home, low-salt canned beef and chicken broth are the best kinds to use. Bouillon cubes and dehydrated broths have a salty,

artificial taste that will affect anything you add them to, no matter how fine the other ingredients may be.

Dried cherries and cranberries: Sun-dried cherries, cranberries, and blueberries are not widely available but they are being used more and more in cooking. Their flavor is intensified by the drying process, and they can be used in sauces, baked goods, and stuffings.

Dried tangerine peel: A classic ingredient in Chinese cooking, dried tangerine or orange peel is available in Asian markets, but you can dry your own easily by cutting strips of zest and letting them dry in sunlight for about a week.

Fish sauce: This salty, savory sauce is used in Thailand, Cambodia, Laos, and Vietnam in the same way as soy sauce is used in China and Japan. Although it may be an acquired taste, it is acquired quickly and can become addictive. Fish sauce is an excellent ingredient for marinades, and it makes an all-purpose dipping sauce when combined with chopped green chilies, a little sugar, and chopped fresh cilantro.

Garlic: We often add garlic to our marinades and sauces, as we think it adds interest and complexity to most dishes. Use fresh garlic, not dried or powdered, which has an artificial taste. To simplify the peeling and chopping of garlic, use a large chef's knife to cut off the root end of each clove, then smash the cloves flat with the side of the knife blade; this makes the skins easy to remove. Chop the cloves by using the French technique of holding the tip of the knife down on the board with your left hand (if you are right-handed) while moving the handle up and down and from left to right with your right hand to chop the cloves evenly. Keep a paring knife at hand to scrape the chopped garlic off the chef's knife periodically.

Ginger: The taste of fresh ginger is incomparable, but ginger root is hard to keep. Even in the refrigerator, it will soften and grow moldy after a couple of weeks. The best solution is to freeze the whole piece of ginger. To use, chop off a piece about the length you think you will use, then mince it with a sharp chef's knife. (You can peel it if you like, but it's not absolutely necessary for most of the recipes in this book.) An even easier method is simply to grate as much of the whole root as the recipe calls for. If you feel like going to more trouble, you can chop the ginger into pieces about 1 inch thick, peel each piece, and put them all into a jar with dry sherry to cover. Keep the jar in the refrigerator and use the flavored sherry in sauces, marinades, and stir-fries.

Hazelnuts: These knobby little morsels are also known as filberts. They have a distinctive mellow flavor that is prized by many cooks. Because they are covered with a papery dark brown skin, they need to be toasted before using; the toasting intensifies their flavor and makes it easier to remove their skins (to toast and peel hazelnuts, see page 85).

Herbs: We like to use fresh herbs when we can, although we have given dried herbs as an alternate to fresh in most of our recipes. The proportion is 3 parts fresh to 1 part dried, as the flavor is concentrated when the herb is dried.

When using fresh herbs, make sure that you strip the leaves or sprigs from the stems and chop only the leaves. The stems are often woody in texture and may also be bitter, as are parsley and basil stems.

Hoisin sauce: Add this sweet-spicy Asian sauce to barbecue sauces and marinades. As a marinade ingredient, it will add an attractive reddish color to grilled foods. Mix hoisin sauce with rice vinegar, Asian sesame oil, and a touch of sugar to make simple sauce for grilled meat.

Hot bean paste: Also called Szechuan hot bean sauce or soybean paste with chili, this fiery paste is available in cans or jars in Asian markets.

Hot chili paste: Made primarily of chilies, salt, oil, and sometimes garlic, bottled chili paste can be found in Asian markets and many large supermarkets. Keep hot chili paste on hand in your refrigerator to use any time you want to add heat and depth to a sauce, marinade, or stir-fry. Chili pastes that contain soybeans are usually called hot bean pastes.

Jalapeño chilies: These small tapered chilies are usually about 3 inches long; they may be either green or red. Serrano chilies, which are smaller and hotter but of a similar shape, may be substituted. Handle fresh chilies with care: Either wear rubber gloves or make sure to wash your hands in hot soapy water right after working with chilies. Remove the seeds, the hottest part, if you're worried about the eventual heat of your sauce or marinade.

Olive paste: A mixture of pureed olives, olive oil, and herbs, this salty, intensely flavored paste is sold in jars in specialty foods stores. With the addition of anchovies and capers it is known as tapenade, which can be substituted for olive paste.

Pancetta: This peppered and rolled Italian bacon is unsmoked, so it can be used to add fat to lean meats without adding a strong flavor. If you can't find it, substitute blanched drained bacon (see page 85).

Parmesan cheese: No Parmesan compares to aged Italian Parmesan, or *parmigiano-reggiano,* in flavor. Highly regulated and controlled by the Italian government, *parmigiano-reggiano* is more expensive than other Parmesans, but the intensity of its taste makes a little go a long way, and it is worth its price. Use a six-sided grater that has a section of miniature shredding holes and grate the Parmesan on this section just before using the grated cheese. Place the piece of Parmesan on a plate with the grater alongside so each person can grate cheese to order at the table.

Rice wine vinegar: A wide variety of alcohol-based Asian vinegars exists, ranging from brown rice vinegar (look for this in natural foods stores) to Chinese black vinegar. They are generally light and fresh, and may be used to balance stronger flavors and bring out the flavor of delicate foods. Try rice vinegar on grilled vegetables, as a marinade ingredient, and as the acidic ingredient in a subtle salad dressing.

Zest: The French distinguish between the *zeste* and the *zist* of citrus fruits, and with good reason: The *zeste* is the thin, colored exterior layer, whose oils contain the intense flavor of the fruit; the *zist* is its bitter white undercoat. Whenever a recipe calls for zest, make sure that you grate only the exterior layer of the citrus fruit and don't go through to the white portion. You can also strip off the zest with a potato peeler or a zester, then mince the zest finely with a chef's knife.

CHAPTER 3

GRILL RECIPES FOR MEATS

New York Steak with Brandy and Black Pepper Sauce

Oven-baked Home Fries · Grilled Whole Shallots
Caesar Salad · Pinot Noir

Serves 4

The tender yet flavorful New York strip steak, cut from the top-loin half of a Porterhouse or T-bone steak, also may be known as a club steak or a Kansas City strip. Cut 1½ inches thick, New York steaks make a deluxe main course for a grill dinner. To give the steaks cross-hatched grill marks, place them at a 45-degree angle to the grids in one direction to grill for the first time on each side; for the second grilling on each side, turn to a 45-degree angle to the grids in the opposite direction. Serve with oven-baked home fries, grilled whole shallots, Caesar salad, and your favorite Pinot Noir.

2 medium shallots, minced
2 tablespoons olive oil
⅓ cup good brandy or Cognac
Four 1½-inch-thick New York strip steaks
   (½ to ¾ pound each)
Black peppercorns in a pepper grinder
½ cup canned low-salt beef broth
2 teaspoons butter
Salt to taste

In a small saucepan, sauté the shallots in the olive oil until they are translucent. Add the brandy or Cognac and bring to a boil over medium heat. Cook and stir the mixture for 2 or 3 minutes over medium heat, then remove from the heat and set aside.

Trim the fat on each steak to no more than ¼ inch thick. Save the fat pieces to grease the cooking rack. Grind the black pepper liberally over both sides of each steak, pressing the pepper into the steak with the back of a spoon. Spread about 1 teaspoon of the oil-brandy mixture evenly over each side of the steaks with the back of a spoon. Let the steaks sit at room temperature for 30 minutes to 1 hour, or cover and refrigerate for 2 to 4 hours. If the steaks have been refrigerated, remove them from the refrigerator just before lighting the charcoal.

Light a charcoal fire in a grill with a hood. When the coals are hot, rub the cooking rack with a piece of reserved fat held with long-handled tongs. Place the steaks on the cooking rack and sear for 2 minutes on each side. Baste with the marinade, turn, cover the grill, and cook the steaks for 3 minutes on each side for rare and 4 minutes for medium rare, basting again before turning the second time (the total cooking time will be 10 minutes for rare and 12 minutes for medium rare).

Transfer the steaks to a plate and cover with aluminum foil. Pour the remaining marinade into a medium saucepan. Add the beef broth to the marinade and bring the mixture to a boil over medium heat. Cook until the sauce is thickened, about 5 minutes. Remove the sauce from the heat and stir in the butter. Add salt to taste. To serve, pour a little of the sauce over each steak.

PORTERHOUSE STEAK WITH
A SAUCE OF SHALLOTS AND JIM BEAM

Shoestring Potatoes · Grilled Tomatoes · Oakleaf Lettuce Salad · Merlot

Serves 3 to 4

The rich taste of Porterhouse steak doesn't need much embellishment; here we've used a simple marinade of shallots, sweet mustard, and bourbon to give the meat an interesting touch of added flavor. Grill summer-ripe halved tomatoes or whole cherry tomatoes just before serving the steak, and accompany it with twice-fried shoestring potatoes and a salad of oakleaf lettuce. Try a good Merlot with this menu.

Two 1½-inch-thick Porterhouse steaks
¼ cup Mendocino mustard or other sweet mustard
¼ cup Jim Beam or other bourbon
3 medium shallots, chopped
Salt to taste

Trim the steaks of all but a ¼-inch edge of fat, reserving the fat to grease the cooking rack. Place the steaks in one layer in a large nonaluminum container. In a small bowl, mix together the mustard, Jim Beam, and shallots. Add salt to taste and spread half of the mixture over the surface of the steaks; turn the steaks and coat the second side. Marinate at room temperature for 30 minutes to 1 hour, or cover and marinate in the refrigerator for 1 to 2 hours, turning the steaks once during this time. If the steaks have been refrigerated, remove them from the refrigerator just before lighting the fire.

Light a charcoal fire in a grill with a hood. When the coals are hot, grease the cooking rack with the reserved fat and sear the steaks for 2 minutes on each side. Cover the grill and cook the steaks for 3 minutes on each side for rare and 4 minutes for medium rare (a total cooking time of 10 minutes for rare and 12 minutes for medium rare). Transfer the steaks to a serving plate and let them sit for 5 minutes before serving.

Grilled Tenderloin of Beef with Fresh Horseradish and Watercress Sauces

Gratin of Artichokes and Potatoes · Butter Lettuce Salad · Cabernet

Serves 4 to 6

The most lavish of all beef cuts, the tenderloin is buttery, mild-flavored, and elegantly simple to cook and serve. A whole tenderloin weighs 4 to 6 pounds and will serve 8 to 12 people; cook it just like the half tenderloin in this recipe. Serve with a gratin of artichokes and potatoes, a butter lettuce salad, and your best Cabernet. For superlative sandwiches, serve leftover cold sliced tenderloin the next day on sliced baguettes, with mild mustard and watercress.

One 2½- to 3-pound tenderloin of beef
3 tablespoons white peppercorns
1 cup crème fraîche, light sour cream, or plain yogurt
2 to 3 tablespoons grated fresh horseradish, or 1
**   tablespoon prepared horseradish (or to taste)**
Salt to taste
1 bunch watercress, stemmed
About 6 tablespoons milk (optional)
Watercress sprigs for garnish

Remove and discard any strings or other ties and trim the tenderloin of all but a ¼-inch layer of fat, reserving the fat to grease the cooking rack. Place the peppercorns on a cutting board and roll a heavy bottle or a rolling pin over them to crush them. Pour the cracked pepper into a shallow nonaluminum container and roll the meat in the pepper to coat the outside of the meat evenly. Let sit at room temperature for 30 minutes to 1 hour.

Using extra coals, light a charcoal fire in a grill with a hood. Using long-handled tongs, grease the cooking rack with the fat. When the coals are hot, sear the tenderloin on each of 3 sides, excluding the fat side, for a total of 10 minutes. Place the meat fat-side down on the side of the cooking rack, cover, and cook for 10 minutes. (Check the fire at this point to make sure it is not burning too slowly; the fire should be hot. If it is not hot enough, shake the grill or stir the coals with a grill utensil and push the coals closer together. Leave the lid off the grill for a few minutes until the fire is burning hot.) Turn the tenderloin, cover the grill, and cook 10 minutes longer (a total cooking time of 30 minutes), or until an instant-read thermometer inserted into the thickest part of the tenderloin reads 140°F for rare. (For medium rare, cook a few minutes longer, to 150°F.)

Transfer the tenderloin from the grill to a carving board and cover with aluminum foil; let it sit while you make the sauces. To make the horseradish sauce: In a small bowl, place ½ cup of the crème fraîche, light sour cream, or yogurt. Add the grated or prepared horseradish and blend well. Add salt to taste and about 3 tablespoons of milk, or enough to make a smooth sauce. To make the watercress sauce: Place the remaining ½ cup crème fraîche, sour cream, or yogurt in a blender or food processor with the watercress and the remaining 3 tablespoons milk and whirl until the watercress is pureed. Add salt to taste and a little more milk as necessary to make a smooth sauce.

Cut the tenderloin into ½-inch-thick slices. Use the two sauces to make a pattern on individual serving plates and place the tenderloin slices on top, or pour a squiggle of each sauce on top of each serving of beef. Garnish the plates with watercress and serve.

GRILLED MARINATED FLANK STEAK WITH SWEET-PEPPER RELISH

Mashed Potatoes · Chicory Salad · Côtes-du-Rhône

Serves 4

Properly grilled and sliced, flank steak is an exception to the rule that the most tender and expensive cuts of beef are best for the grill. A simple marinade complements the rich taste of flank steak. Serve with mashed potatoes, chicory salad, our cooked relish of sweet bell peppers, and a Côtes-du-Rhône. If you have leftovers, cold grilled flank steak makes wonderful next-day sandwiches with a sharp mustard, black bread, and slivered green onions.

One 1½-pound flank steak

Marinade

1 cup dry red wine
3 tablespoons olive oil
2 tablespoons hoisin sauce
1 tablespoon grated fresh ginger
1 tablespoon hot chili paste
¼ teaspoon Asian sesame oil
3 or 4 garlic cloves, cut into ovals

Sweet-Pepper Relish

2 red bell peppers, cored, seeded, and chopped
1 small white onion, chopped
Pinch of dried red pepper flakes
½ teaspoon mustard seed
Salt to taste
½ cup brown sugar or to taste
⅓ cup white wine vinegar
About ¾ cup water

With the dull side of a chef's knife or other heavy knife, pound the flank steak crosswise several times on each side. Place the steak in a shallow nonaluminum container. Combine the marinade ingredients and pour the marinade over the steak. Let sit at room temperature for at least 30 minutes or up to 2 hours, or marinate in the refrigerator for 2 to 4 hours. Turn the flank steak 3 or 4 times while it is marinating. If the steak has been refrigerated, remove it from the refrigerator just before lighting the fire.

Light a charcoal fire in an open grill. While the coals are heating, make the relish: In a medium nonaluminum pan, combine all the ingredients for the relish, bring to a boil, reduce the heat to low, and simmer until the peppers are translucent and the relish has thickened, about 30 minutes, adding more water during cooking as necessary. Adjust the level of sweetness as you like, and let cool to room temperature.

When the coals are hot, place the flank steak bottom-side down (the top is the side with connective tissue) on the cooking rack and cook for 6 minutes. Baste, turn, and cook for 6 minutes on the second side (a total cooking time of 12 minutes for medium rare). Transfer from the grill to a carving board and cover the flank steak with a plate or aluminum foil for 5 to 10 minutes.

Using a sharp slicing knife held at a 45-degree angle, and beginning at the thin end of the steak, cut the steak crosswise into ¼-inch-thick diagonal slices. Place the slices on a serving plate. Pour any juices from the carving board over the sliced steak and serve with the relish alongside.

ALDER-SMOKED BRISKET WITH CHILI PASTE AND SMOKED-TOMATO SALSA

Fresh-corn Pancakes · Italian Green Beans · Microbrewed Beer or Ale

Serves 12 to 14

Brisket isn't usually thought of as grill fare, but this slightly chewy, flavorful cut is excellent cooked either rare or well done, then cut into thin slices. Because it's relatively inexpensive and comes in large pieces, it's a good choice for entertaining a group. Buy the section called the "flat cut," which also comes in smaller sizes (buy a brisket half the size below to serve 6 or 7 people).

Brisket is complemented by assertive flavors, so we've added the taste of alder smoke, a spicy chili paste, and a *picante* salsa of smoked tomato and jalapeño. Fresh-corn pancakes and Italian green beans are good companions. This recipe is also good for large picnic gatherings, as thin slices of brisket make great sandwiches to serve on country bread with potato salad or coleslaw. To drink: your favorite locally microbrewed beer or ale.

One 3½- to 4-pound beef brisket (flat cut)

Chili Paste

2 tablespoons olive oil
1 tablespoon red wine vinegar
5 garlic cloves
1 tablespoon chili powder
1 teaspoon paprika
½ teaspoon cayenne
1 teaspoon cumin
Juice of ½ lime
¼ cup fresh cilantro leaves
½ onion, coarsely chopped
Salt to taste
Water as necessary for blending

1 cup alder or hickory chips

Smoked-Tomato Salsa

2 large ripe tomatoes
2 jalapeño chilies
Juice of ½ lime
1 teaspoon olive oil
Salt to taste
3 tablespoons chopped fresh cilantro

Trim the brisket of all but a ¼-inch layer of fat and reserve some of the fat to grease the cooking rack. Place the brisket in a large, shallow nonaluminum container. To make the chili paste, place all of the ingredients in a blender or food processor and blend to a smooth paste. Spread the paste evenly on both sides of the brisket and let sit at room temperature for 2 hours, or cover and place in the refrigerator for 2 to 4 hours. If the brisket has been refrigerated, remove it from the refrigerator just before lighting the coals.

Using extra coals, light a charcoal fire in a grill with a hood, using charcoal baskets or charcoal rails if you have them. While the coals are heating, place the alder or hickory chips in water to cover. When the coals are hot, push half of them to either side of the grill if you have not used baskets or rails.

Grease the cooking rack with the reserved fat, using long-handled tongs. Place the brisket, fat-side up, in the center of the cooking rack and sear for 5 minutes. Drain the wood chips and sprinkle them evenly over the coals. Turn the brisket, cover the grill, partially close the top vents (leave the bottom vents open), and cook for 15 minutes. Check once or twice during this period to make sure the fire isn't dying down; if it is, stir or shake the coals and open the top vents completely. Turn the brisket, cover the grill, and cook another 15 minutes for medium rare (a total cooking time of 35 minutes). If you prefer your meat well done, turn the brisket again and cook 15 minutes longer, for a total of 50 minutes.

Meanwhile, during the last 15 minutes of cooking the brisket, make the salsa: Place the tomatoes on one side of the cooking rack. Cook until the tomatoes are soft and slightly charred; remove from the grill and let cool. Remove the brisket, when done, to a carving board, cover with aluminum foil, and let sit for 10 minutes.

Meanwhile, stem and chop the smoked tomatoes and place in a small bowl. Mince the jalapeños (retain the seeds if you like a hot sauce) and add them to the tomatoes in the bowl along with all the remaining salsa ingredients.

Cut the brisket crosswise into very thin diagonal slices and pile the slices on a serving plate. Serve the salsa alongside.

BEEF SATAY WITH JAPANESE EGGPLANT AND PEANUT SAUCE

Fresh Rice Flour Noodles · Bean Sprout and Grated Carrot Salad with Cilantro
Asian Beer

Serves 4

Peanut sauce is one of the great culinary inventions. Savory, spicy, sweet, and hot all at the same time, its complex, rich flavor is magic with chicken, vegetables, tofu, and especially with threaded slices of tender beef and chunks of Japanese eggplant grilled over charcoal. Serve with fresh rice flour noodles, a bean sprout and grated carrot salad with cilantro, and a good Asian beer.

1 pound beef sirloin tip, cut into ¼-inch-thick slices
3 or 4 Japanese eggplants, halved and cut into
    1-inch pieces

Peanut Sauce

½ cup unsalted smooth peanut butter
2 tablespoons low-salt soy sauce
⅓ cup minced fresh cilantro
4 garlic cloves, minced
1 tablespoon minced fresh ginger
Juice of 1 lemon
1 teaspoon dried red pepper flakes
¼ cup peanut oil
1 teaspoon fish sauce
¼ cup rice wine vinegar
¼ cup water or more
Cayenne to taste (optional)

If you are using wooden skewers, soak them for at least 30 minutes in water to cover. Thread the sirloin tip slices lengthwise on long metal or water-soaked wooden skewers, alternating the meat with lengthwise pieces of Japanese eggplant, and place the skewers in a shallow nonaluminum container.

To make the peanut sauce: In a medium bowl, blender, or food processor, combine all of the ingredients except the cayenne and blend to a smooth sauce; add more water for a thinner sauce. Taste for seasoning and add cayenne to taste, if you like.

Brush the meat liberally with the peanut sauce, then turn and brush the other side. Marinate the meat at room temperature for 1 or 2 hours, or cover and refrigerate for 2 to 4 hours, turning the meat once or twice during this period. If refrigerated, remove the skewers from the refrigerator just before lighting the fire.

Light a charcoal fire in an open grill. When the coals are hot, cook the skewers for 2 to 3 minutes on each side. Serve the meat on the skewers, accompanied with a bowl of peanut sauce for dipping.

KOREAN BARBECUED BEEF WITH GRILLED BABY LEEKS AND GINGER DIPPING SAUCE

Cold Sesame Spinach · Steamed Rice · Kim Chee
Asian Beer

Serves 4

A sweet-hot marinade and the magic of the grill will turn short ribs into a special treat. Have your butcher cut short ribs crosswise through the bone into ¼-inch-thick slices. On the grill, the fat will melt away, leaving the savory, slightly chewy meat, which you may find addictive. Eat around the small pieces of bone, dipping the grilled meat into the refreshing sauce—you'll find it a perfect complement to the spicy marinade. Serve with cold sesame spinach, steamed rice, and kim chee (this hot, hot Korean favorite is most often made from cabbage, but many other kinds of these chili-fermented vegetable relishes exist; try several varieties of kim chee if you can find them). Serve with Asian beer.

3 to 4 pounds short ribs, cut crosswise into
  ¼-inch-thick slices
½ cup peanut oil
¼ cup soy sauce
1 teaspoon sesame seeds
1 teaspoon Asian sesame oil
2 green onions, chopped
3 garlic cloves, chopped
1 to 2 teaspoons hot chili paste
1½ tablespoons brown sugar
½ cup rice wine vinegar
16 to 20 baby leeks, halved leeks, green garlics, or
  green onions
Olive oil for coating

Dipping Sauce

1 cup rice wine vinegar
2 tablespoons chopped fresh cilantro
2 teaspoons chopped fresh ginger

Place the short rib slices in several layers in a large, shallow nonaluminum container. In a medium bowl, mix together all the ingredients for the marinade and pour over the short ribs. Let sit for 2 hours at room temperature, or cover and marinate for 4 to 8 hours or overnight in the refrigerator, turning the short ribs 3 or 4 times during this period. If the short ribs have been refrigerated, remove them from the refrigerator just before lighting the charcoal.

Light a charcoal fire in an open grill. While the coals are heating, place the leeks, green garlics, or green onions in a shallow container and pour a little olive oil over them; using your hands, coat them all over with the oil.

When the coals are hot, place the leeks, garlics, or onions on one side of the cooking rack; place the short ribs in the center (use a grill basket for the short ribs if you have one). Grill the vegetables until lightly charred on each side; grill the meat for 4 minutes on each side.

Transfer the vegetables and meat from the grill to a serving plate or individual plates. Combine all of the ingredients for the dipping sauce. Divide the dipping sauce evenly among 4 small bowls and serve one to each diner along with the meat and vegetables.

STEAK FAJITAS WITH GRILLED-PAPAYA SALSA

Green Rice with Poblano Chilies · Avocado Salad · Hot Corn Tortillas
Mexican Beer

Serves 4

Steak fajitas are usually made from the skirt steak, a rather chewy piece of meat that benefits from long marinating. You can substitute another lean steak, of course, such as sirloin or round steak. Unlike the skirt steak, these cuts will not need to be slashed, and will need to be marinated for only an hour or so at room temperature. Cut the steak into thin slices after grilling. Accompany the fajitas with green rice made with poblano chilies, an avocado salad, hot corn tortillas, and grilled-papaya salsa. (If you have access to handmade tortillas, they are worth a special shopping trip for this meal.) Serve your favorite Mexican beer alongside.

1 pound skirt steak

Marinade

Juice of 2 limes
3 unseeded red jalapeño or serrano chilies, minced
1 tablespoon olive oil
¼ teaspoon ground black pepper
Salt to taste
¼ cup minced fresh cilantro

2 tablespoons olive oil
2 tablespoons lime juice or to taste
1 papaya, peeled, seeded, and cut into
  1-inch-thick wedges
8 corn tortillas, preferably handmade
1 red jalapeño or serrano chili, seeded and minced
1 small white onion, chopped
2 tablespoons chopped fresh cilantro
Salt to taste

With a sharp knife, make 1-inch-deep diagonal cuts every 2 inches on both sides of the skirt steak. Combine all the ingredients for the marinade in a large, shallow nonaluminum container. Add the steak, turning it to coat both sides with the marinade. Cover and place in the refrigerator for 4 to 8 hours, or overnight, turning the steak 3 or 4 times during this period. If the steak has been refrigerated, remove it from the refrigerator just before lighting the fire.

Light a charcoal fire in an open grill. While the coals are heating, begin making the salsa: In a medium bowl, combine the olive oil and 2 tablespoons of the lime juice. Place the papaya wedges in the bowl and coat them on all side with the oil-lime mixture. Place the papaya wedges on a grill grid, on a piece of metal screening, or in a grill basket, reserving the oil-lime mixture and juice left in the bowl.

When the coals are hot, brush each tortilla lightly with water and place all the tortillas in a stack. Cover the tortillas with aluminum foil and place the packet on one side of the cooking rack.

Grill the steak for 3 to 4 minutes. Baste the steak with the marinade, turn, baste it again, and grill another 3 to 4 minutes (a total cooking time of 6 to 8 minutes). Transfer the steak from the grill to a carving board, cover with aluminum foil, and let sit while you finish heating the tortillas and making the salsa.

Turn the tortilla packet to heat on the other side. Place the papaya wedges on the grill and cook them for 2 to 3 minutes per side, or until lightly charred. Remove the papayas from the grill, chop them coarsely, and place them back in the bowl with the oil-lime mixture. Add the chili, onion, cilantro, and salt to taste. Taste and add a little more lime juice, if you like.

Chop the steak into bits with a cleaver or a large, heavy knife. Fill 2 hot tortillas per person with chopped steak and a little salsa, or place the plate of chopped steak, the tortillas, and the salsa on the table and let the diners help themselves.

VARIATIONS ON THE PERFECT HAMBURGER

Guacamole · Marinated Red Onion Rings
Grilled Whole Baby Red Potatoes · Green Salad · Choice of Beers

Each recipe serves 4; all 3 recipes together serve 12

Three different groups of flavorful additions make delicious variations on the basic hamburger. We like our hamburgers served on bakery-fresh Kaiser or sourdough rolls, with romaine lettuce leaves, a mixture of Dijon mustard and mayonnaise, and/or an assortment of toppings such as guacamole, marinated red onion rings, and goat cheese. Or try a variety of mustards: mustard with garlic, mustard with chilies, herb mustard, sweet Mendocino mustard, and so on. The time given below will result in medium-rare meat; adjust the cooking time accordingly if you like your hamburgers rare or well done. Grilled whole baby red potatoes and a big green salad are good side dishes; serve a choice of two or three kinds of beer to go along with the different hamburgers.

Far East Hamburgers

1½ pounds ground chuck
2 teaspoons minced garlic
2 teaspoons grated fresh ginger
2 teaspoons minced jalapeño chili
2 teaspoons low-salt soy sauce
Pinch of salt

Mediterranean Hamburgers

1½ pounds ground chuck
1 tablespoon chopped pine nuts
1 tablespoon freshly grated Parmesan cheese
1 tablespoon fine dry bread crumbs
1 teaspoon minced garlic
1 teaspoon olive oil
Pinch of salt

Blue Cheese Hamburgers

1½ pounds ground chuck
3 or 4 medium shallots, chopped
½ cup crumbled blue cheese
Pinch of salt

12 freshly baked Kaiser or sourdough rolls, halved
Assorted garnishes: romaine lettuce leaves, various mustards, Dijon mustard mixed with mayonnaise, crumbled or sliced goat cheese, Guacamole (following), Marinated Red Onion Rings (following)

Light a charcoal fire in a grill with a hood. While the coals are heating, mix together all the ingredients for each recipe in separate medium bowls. Let sit at room temperature until the coals are hot, 30 to 45 minutes.

When the coals are hot, form the meat for each recipe into 4 loosely molded patties. Make sure the grill rack is clean (scrub it with a wire grill brush to make sure) and well oiled, or use a grill basket for the hamburgers. Cook the hamburgers on each side for 2 minutes. Place the halved buns cut-side down on the edges of the grill rack.

Turn the hamburgers, cover the grill, and cook the hamburgers for 2 minutes on each side (a total cooking time of 8 minutes for medium rare), or until they are done to your preference and the buns are lightly toasted. Transfer the buns from the grill to a plate, add the hamburgers to the buns, and serve with the optional toppings.

Guacamole

In a medium bowl, mash 1 peeled and seeded avocado with a fork. Add 2 minced small garlic cloves, and fresh lemon juice, salt, and Tabasco sauce to taste. Let sit, tightly covered, at room temperature for 30 minutes to 1 hour. Serves 4.

Marinated Red Onion Rings

Peel 2 large red onions and cut them into thin slices. Place the slices in a medium bowl and separate them into rings. Add 1 tablespoon canola or other vegetable oil and ¼ cup white wine vinegar. Sprinkle lightly with salt and a pinch of sugar. Mix together gently with a wooden spoon and let sit at room temperature for 30 minutes to 1 hour. A sprinkling of cayenne and/or chopped fresh flat-leaf parsley or cilantro is optional. Serves 4.

RACK OF LAMB MARINATED IN POMEGRANATE JUICE AND SERVED WITH FRESH-MINT SAUCE

Grilled Carrots and Zucchini · Couscous with Golden Raisins and Pistachios
Gewürztraminer or Riesling

Serves 4 to 6

In this Middle Eastern–inspired recipe, the lamb is marinated in a dark, fruity marinade and served with a quickly made puree of fresh mint. If you can't find or make pomegranate juice, cranberry-raspberry juice makes a good substitute. The pomegranate syrup or port adds a deeper note to the marinade, but is not necessary. The combination of sweet and spicy flavors makes this a very special grill dish to serve with couscous with golden raisins and pistachios, and grilled carrots and zucchini (cut 1 or 2 trimmed carrots and zucchini per person into ¼-inch-thick *lengthwise* slices, coat with olive oil, and grill with the lamb until lightly charred and tender). Accompany with a chilled, spicy white wine such as Gewürztraminer or Riesling.

Two 8-rib racks of lamb

Marinade

3 cups fresh or bottled pomegranate juice★
    or cranberry-raspberry juice
¼ cup pomegranate syrup, ruby port, or
    grenadine (optional)
¼ cup olive oil
Juice of 1 lemon (with pomegranate juice) or orange
    (with cranberry-raspberry juice)
6 garlic cloves
Ground white pepper to taste
Salt to taste

Fresh-Mint Sauce

1 cup fresh mint leaves, packed (about 2 bunches mint)
½ cup fresh parsley sprigs, packed
Juice of 1 lemon
2 tablespoons olive oil
¼ teaspoon sugar
Cayenne to taste
Salt to taste
Water as necessary for pureeing

Trim the lamb of all but a ¼-inch layer of fat. Reserve the fat to grease the cooking rack. Place the racks of lamb in a large nonaluminum bowl. In a medium bowl, mix all the ingredients for the marinade together and pour over the lamb. Cover and marinate for 4 to 8 hours or overnight in the refrigerator, turning the lamb 3 or 4 times during this period. Remove the lamb from the refrigerator just before lighting the coals.

Light a charcoal fire in a grill with a hood. When the coals are hot, grease the cooking rack with the reserved fat, using long-handled tongs. Sear the lamb for 3 minutes on each side. Place the lamb fat-side down at one side of the cooking rack and cover the grill. Cook for 10 minutes, then baste with the marinade, turn, cover the grill, and cook for 10 to 15 minutes on the second side for medium rare (a total cooking time of 26 to 31 minutes), or until an instant-read thermometer inserted in the center of a rack reads 150°F.

Transfer the lamb from the grill to a carving board, cover it with aluminum foil, and let it sit for 10 minutes. Meanwhile, make the mint sauce: Place all the ingredients for the sauce in a blender or food processor and puree, adding a little water as necessary to create a smooth sauce. Cut the lamb into ribs and serve accompanied with the mint sauce.

★Look for bottled pomegranate juice in natural foods stores. Fresh pomegranate juice is even better. Make your own in the fall and early winter when pomegranates are in season: Cut the promegranates in half crosswise and squeeze them in a juicer (take care to protect your clothing, as the juice will stain).

OLIVE WOOD–SMOKED SADDLE OF LAMB
WITH OLIVE PASTE AND AÏOLI

Braised Baby Artichokes · Herbed Focaccia · Chianti Classico or Rioja

Serves 6 to 8

A combination of Mediterranean flavors makes this an inspired choice for a grill meal: Olive paste is blended with fresh herbs and used to coat the lamb, and the scented smoke of olive wood adds flavor to the grilled meat, which is served with aïoli. The saddle of lamb, which consists of boned double loin chops rolled and tied, is easy to cook and serve, so it is an especially good cut for entertaining. For a dinner for 3 or 4 people, buy a boned single loin (about 1½ pounds).

Serve the lamb cut into slices on a bed of braised baby artichokes, with herbed focaccia and aïoli alongside, and a Chianti Classico or a Rioja.

> One 3¼-pound saddle of lamb
> Salt and freshly ground black pepper to taste
> ¼ cup olive paste
> 2 tablespoons olive oil
> 2 tablespoons chopped fresh thyme or rosemary, or 2 teaspoons crumbled dried thyme or rosemary (or to taste)
> 1 cup olive wood chips

Aïoli

> 1 extra-large egg
> 4 garlic cloves, smashed or forced through a garlic press
> ¼ teaspoon salt
> 1½ cups mild or light olive oil, or 1 cup olive oil and ½ cup canola oil, at room temperature
> 1 tablespoon white wine vinegar
> Juice of ½ lemon (about 2 tablespoons), or to taste
> Cayenne to taste

Trim the lamb of all but a ¼-inch layer of fat, reserving the fat to grease the cooking rack. Unroll the saddle and sprinkle the inside evenly with salt and pepper. In a small bowl, combine the olive paste, oil, and herbs. Spread this mixture evenly over the inside and outside of the lamb, and rub it into the meat with your fingers. Roll the lamb up and tie it in 4 or 5 places with cotton string.

Place the lamb in a shallow nonaluminum container and let it sit at room temperature for 1 hour, or cover and place in the refrigerator for 1 to 2 hours. If the lamb has been refrigerated, remove it from the refrigerator just before you light the coals.

Using extra coals, light a charcoal fire in a grill with a hood, using charcoal baskets or charcoal rails if you have them. Place the olive chips in water to cover. When the coals are red hot, if you have not used baskets or rails, divide the coals in half and push them to opposite sides of the grill. Place a metal baking pan in the center of the fuel bed between the coals to act as a drip pan.

Grease the cooking rack with the reserved fat, using long-handled tongs. Place the lamb in the center of the cooking rack over the drip pan and sear for 2 or 3 minutes on each of all 4 sides (a total of 10 minutes). Drain the olive chips well and sprinkle them evenly over the coals. Partially close the vents, cover the grill, and cook the lamb for 15 minutes. Turn, cover the grill, and cook on the second side for 20 minutes (a total cooking time of 45 minutes for rare lamb), or until an instant-read thermometer inserted in the center of the roast reads 140°F; cook a few minutes longer, or until the thermometer reads 150°F, for medium rare. Transfer the lamb from the grill to a carving board and cover it with aluminum foil; let sit for 15 to 20 minutes.

While the lamb is cooking, make the aïoli: Place the egg in a medium, deep bowl and add hot water to cover to warm the egg; set aside for 10 minutes. Remove the egg from the bowl, pour out the hot water, and dry the bowl with a towel. Fold the towel and place it under the bowl to hold it steady when you whisk in the oil. With a wooden pestle or the bottom of a small bottle, grind the garlic and salt together to make a smooth paste. Beat the egg into the mixture with a whisk until well blended.

Holding the whisk in one hand and the oil in the other, very gradually beat in the oil just a few drops at a time until the mixture thickens and lightens somewhat in color. At this point, begin adding the oil a little faster while whisking it into the mixture, until all the oil has been added. Whisk in the wine vinegar and then the lemon juice; adjust the seasoning with vinegar, lemon juice, and salt. Add cayenne to taste. Place the aïoli in a covered container and refrigerate until the lamb is ready to serve; the sauce will thicken slightly.

Slice the lamb into serving pieces and serve on a bed of braised baby artichokes with the aïoli alongside.

Grilled Butterflied Leg of Lamb with Indian Spices and Cucumber Chutney

Masoor Dal · Braised Spinach
Iced Indian Tea, Beer, or Chilled Rosé

Serves 8

A grill dinner in the great tradition of Indian lamb cookery: a butterflied leg of lamb rubbed with an aromatic dry spice mix, grilled flat, and served with a cool chutney with a touch of fresh chili. This cut of lamb is a good choice for company, because the different thicknesses of the meat will give your guests a range of doneness. The spice mix is our version of garam masala, a classic Indian flavoring blend. You might want to make up a large quantity and keep it in an airtight jar, as it is equally good on grilled fish and chicken, and it's also nice with braised or sautéed lamb or chicken. You also may buy prepared garam masala in specialty foods stores. Serve the sliced lamb on a bed of masoor dal (spiced red lentils), accompanied with braised spinach. To drink: iced Indian tea, cold beer, or a chilled rosé.

One 4-pound butterflied leg of lamb
Olive oil

Garam Masala

⅓ **cup ground coriander**
1 **tablespoon ground cumin**
1 **teaspoon ground cinnamon**
¼ **teaspoon cayenne**
¼ **teaspoon salt**
¼ **teaspoon ground nutmeg**
⅛ **teaspoon ground cloves**
⅛ **teaspoon ground cardamom**

Cucumber Chutney

1 **cup minced English cucumber**
½ **cup minced white onion**
Juice of ½ lime
½ **jalapeño chili, seeded and minced**
¼ **cup minced fresh cilantro**
¼ **cup plain yogurt**
Salt to taste

Cilantro sprigs for garnish

Trim the lamb of all but a ¼-inch layer of fat; pull off any fell (a thin membrane often found on lamb). Place the lamb in a shallow nonaluminum container and rub the meat all over with olive oil. In a small bowl, combine all the ingredients for the masala, then sprinkle the masala evenly on both sides of the lamb and rub it into the meat with your hands. Let the lamb sit at room temperature for 1 hour, or cover and place in the refrigerator for 2 hours. If the lamb has been refrigerated, remove it from the refrigerator just before you light the fire.

Light a charcoal fire in a grill with a cover. While the coals are heating, make the cucumber chutney: In a small bowl, combine all the ingredients and let sit at room temperature until the lamb is ready to serve.

When the coals are hot, sear the lamb for 3 minutes on each side. Cover the grill and cook the lamb for 12 minutes, then turn, cover, and cook for another 12 minutes (a total cooking time of 30 minutes), or until an instant-read thermometer inserted in the thickest part of the meat reads 150°F. This part of the lamb will be medium rare, and the thinner parts will be medium. Transfer the lamb from the grill to a carving board and cover with aluminum foil; let sit for 10 minutes.

Cut the lamb into slices and serve over a bed of dal. (Reserve the juice from the lamb and pass it in a little pitcher, if you like.) Serve with the cucumber chutney and garnish with cilantro sprigs.

Lamb Kabobs with Summer Vegetables, Bay Leaves, and Garlic-Yogurt Sauce

Rice Pilaf · Spinach Salad · Warm Pita Breads
Beer, or White or Red Wine

Serves 4

This classic Mediterranean dish includes zucchini or summer squash, onions, bell peppers, and bay leaves, and is served with a pungent garlic-yogurt sauce. Served with rice pilaf and a spinach salad, it's a perfect summer grill meal, and a good one to choose for picnics. Make the kabobs and place them, along with the marinade, in a nonaluminum container with a tight-fitting top. Pack the kabobs, sauce, salad, and salad dressing in a cooler along with beer or your favorite white or red wine, and take off for the beach, a ballgame, or a camping trip.

12 whole baby squash, or 3 to 4 zucchini or summer squash
1½ pounds boneless leg of lamb, trimmed of fat and cut into 1½-inch cubes
Twelve 1-inch-diameter boiling onions, peeled, or 1-inch chunks of white onion
1 *each* red and yellow bell pepper, cored, seeded, and cut into eighths
16 whole fresh bay (laurel) leaves, or dried bay leaves soaked in warm water for 30 minutes

Marinade

2 tablespoons oil
Juice of ½ lemon
1 teaspoon ground cumin
Salt, ground white pepper, and cayenne to taste
2 tablespoons minced fresh parsley

Garlic-Yogurt Sauce

1 cup plain yogurt
2 or 3 medium garlic cloves, minced
Salt to taste

Pita breads

Leave the baby squash whole if they are quite small, otherwise cut them in half. Cut the zucchini or summer squash in half lengthwise, then into 1½-inch pieces. Thread the lamb and vegetables on long skewers, alternating the lamb, vegetables, and whole bay leaves. Place the skewers flat in a shallow nonaluminum container. Mix together all the ingredients for the marinade and pour it over the skewers. Marinate at room temperature for 30 minutes to 2 hours, or cover and marinate in the refrigerator for 2 to 4 hours; turn the skewers 3 or 4 times during this period. If the kabobs have been refrigerated, remove them from the refrigerator just before you light the coals.

Light a charcoal fire in a grill with a hood. While the coals are heating, prepare the garlic-yogurt sauce: In a medium nonaluminum bowl, mix together all the ingredients and let sit at room temperature to develop the flavors.

When the coals are hot, sear the kabobs for 2 minutes on each side, then baste and turn, using long-handled tongs. Cover the grill and cook for 3 minutes. Baste, turn, cover the grill, and cook for 3 minutes on the second side (a total cooking time of 10 minutes for medium-rare lamb).

Transfer the kabobs from the grill to a plate and cover with aluminum foil. Let sit while warming the pita breads for a few minutes on each side in the covered grill, then serve accompanied with a bowl of garlic-yogurt sauce and the warm pita breads.

GRILLED PORK CHOPS WITH FRESH TOMATO-PEPPER RELISH

Spinach Gnocchi · Grilled Summer Squash · Barbaresco or Barolo

Serves 4

Grilled thick pork chops scented with fresh thyme make a perfect summer meal; accompany with spinach gnocchi, grilled summer squash, and our fresh relish of chopped tomatoes and sweet yellow peppers. To drink: a Barbaresco or Barolo.

Four 1½-inch-thick center-cut pork loin chops

Marinade

1 tablespoon olive oil
1 teaspoon red wine vinegar
2 medium garlic cloves, minced
1 tablespoon chopped fresh thyme, or 1 teaspoon
   crumbled dried thyme
Thyme stems and sprigs for the fire (optional)

Fresh Tomato-Pepper Relish

2 vine-ripened tomatoes, 8 Roma tomatoes,
  or 1 basket cherry tomatoes, chopped
1 white onion, minced
1 large yellow bell pepper, cored, seeded, and chopped
1 tablespoon chopped fresh flat-leaf parsley
2 teaspoons olive oil
2 teaspoons white wine vinegar
1 teaspoon balsamic vinegar
Salt to taste
Ground white pepper to taste

Fresh thyme sprigs for garnish (optional)

Place the pork chops in one layer in a shallow non-aluminum container. Mix together the marinade ingredients and pour the mixture over the pork chops. Marinate for 30 minutes to 2 hours at room temperature, or cover and marinate for 2 to 4 hours in the refrigerator, turning the chops 2 or 3 times during this period. If the chops have been refrigerated, remove them from the refrigerator just before you light the fire.

Light a charcoal fire in a grill with a cover. Place any leftover thyme stems and a few sprigs in water to cover, if you want to add them to the fire. While the coals are heating, prepare the relish: In a medium ceramic or glass bowl, combine all the ingredients and let sit at room temperature until the pork chops are ready to serve, stirring the relish once or twice during this period.

When the coals are hot, sear the pork chops for 4 minutes on each side. Drain the thyme stems and sprigs, if using, and sprinkle them evenly over the hot coals. Baste the chops with the marinade, turn, cover the grill, and cook the chops for 3 minutes; then baste and turn the chops again, cover the grill, and cook the chops for another 3 minutes (a total cooking time of 14 minutes), or until an instant-read thermometer inserted into the center of a chop reads 150°F.

Transfer the chops to a serving plate or individual plates and let sit for 5 minutes. Place a serving of relish alongside each chop; garnish with thyme sprigs, if you like, and serve.

GRILLED PORK TENDERLOINS WITH APPLE-SHERRY SAUCE

Baked Garlic Grits · Wilted Salad · Moselle

Serves 4

This grill dish is elegant enough for a candlelight dinner and is a good choice for cool fall evenings or any time you crave the classic flavor combination of pork and apples. Grilling the tenderloins over apple wood chunks gives them an extra tang of sweet smoke. Serve with a casserole of baked garlic grits, a wilted salad, and a Moselle wine.

2 pork tenderloins (a total of about 1¾ to 2 pounds)

Marinade

2 shallots
½ cup medium-dry sherry
¼ cup olive oil
Salt and black pepper to taste

1 cup apple wood chips

Apple-Sherry Sauce

1 tablespoon butter
1 tablespoon olive oil
3 shallots, chopped
2 tart apples, peeled, cored, and minced
¼ cup light cream or half-and-half
¼ cup medium-dry sherry
½ cup unfiltered apple juice
2 tablespoons fresh lemon juice, or to taste
Salt and ground white pepper to taste

Place the tenderloins in a shallow nonaluminum container. In a small bowl, combine all the ingredients for the marinade and pour it over the tenderloins, turning them to coat on all sides. Let marinate for 1 to 2 hours at room temperature, or cover and refrigerate for 2 to 4 hours, turning the meat 2 or 3 times during this period. If the meat has been refrigerated, remove it from the refrigerator just before lighting the coals.

Light a charcoal fire in a grill with a hood. Place the wood chips in water to cover. While the coals are heating, make the sauce: In a medium sauté pan or skillet, melt the butter with the olive oil and sauté the shallots until they are translucent. Add the chopped apples and sauté for 2 or 3 minutes, then stir in the cream or half-and-half, sherry, apple juice, and lemon juice, and cook over medium heat for 10 or 12 minutes, or until the apples are tender and the sauce is slightly thickened. Add more lemon juice to taste, if you like. Season to taste with salt and pepper and set aside.

When the coals are hot, sear the tenderloins for 3 minutes on each side. Baste with the marinade, turn, cover the grill, and cook for 5 minutes; baste, turn, cover the grill and cook another 5 minutes (a total of 16 minutes for medium rare), or until an instant-read thermometer inserted in the thickest part of a tenderloin reads 150°F.

Transfer the tenderloins from the grill to a carving board and cover with aluminum foil; let sit for 5 or 10 minutes. Meanwhile, bring the sauce to a simmer until heated through. Cut the tenderloins into ½-inch-thick slices. Pool the warm sauce on each plate and top with slices of tenderloin.

GRILLED PORK LOIN WITH WARM DRIED-FRUIT COMPOTE

Warm Cabbage Salad · Scalloped Potatoes · Zinfandel

Serves 4 to 6

This savory dish is good any time, but is an especially good choice for grilling on fall and mild winter days. The dried-fruit marinade is cooked into a warm compote to serve alongside the sliced pork. Serve with a warm cabbage salad, scalloped potatoes, and a good Zinfandel.

One 2½-pound boneless pork loin roast

Marinade

1 dozen whole dried apricots
1 dozen dried figs or prunes
1 dozen dried pears
⅓ cup dried cranberries or golden raisins
1 cup dry white wine
1 tablespoon fresh lemon juice
1 tablespoon brown sugar
2 tablespoons olive oil
3 garlic cloves, cut into ovals
Zest of 1 lemon, cut into shreds

Trim the pork loin of all but a ¼-inch layer of fat, reserving the fat to grease the cooking rack. Place the roast in a shallow nonaluminum container. Mix together all of the marinade ingredients and pour over the roast. Marinate the roast at room temperature for 1 to 2 hours, or cover and marinate in the refrigerator for 2 to 4 hours, turning the roast 2 or 3 times during this period. If the roast has been refrigerated, remove it from the refrigerator just before lighting the coals.

Light a charcoal fire in a grill with a hood. When the coals are hot, grease the cooking rack with the reserved fat, using long-handled tongs, and sear the roast for 2 to 3 minutes on each of all 4 sides, for a total cooking time of 10 minutes. Baste the roast with the marinade, move it to one side of the cooking rack, and cover the grill; cook for 15 minutes. Baste and turn the roast again, keeping it to one side of the cooking rack. Cover the grill and cook the roast for 10 to 15 minutes (a total cooking time of 35 to 40 minutes), or until the meat is barely pink in the center or an instant-read thermometer inserted into the center of the roast registers 150°F.

Meanwhile, after turning the roast the second time, pour all the marinade ingredients into a medium saucepan, bring to a simmer, and cook until the mixture has thickened and the fruit is plumped, about 20 minutes; set aside.

Transfer the roast from the grill to a carving board and cover it with aluminum foil; let sit for 15 to 20 minutes. Just before serving, heat the sauce over low heat until it is warmed through. Cut the roast into ½-inch-thick slices, pour any juice from the roast over the slices, and serve with the warm fruit compote alongside.

CROWN ROAST OF PORK
WITH A SAUCE OF CHERRIES, CREAM, AND PORT

Onions Braised in Balsamic Vinegar with Bay Leaves · Fennel Salad with Orange Slices · Merlot

Serves 14 to 16

The crown roast is an extravagant cut of meat that's perfect for a large dinner for a special occasion such as Thanksgiving or Christmas. Serve the roast stuffed with wild rice and accompany it with onions braised in balsamic vinegar with bay leaves, fennel salad with orange slices, and a fine Merlot.

2 tablespoons olive oil
2 tablespoons red wine vinegar
One 18-rib crown roast of pork (8 to 8½ pounds)
Salt and ground white pepper to taste
2 or 3 tablespoons dried thyme or sage

Cherry, Port, and Cream Sauce

½ cup fresh, dried, or frozen cherries or cranberries, minced (fresh cherries should be pitted)
Juice of 1 lemon
1 tablespoon butter
3 large shallots, minced
1 cup half-and-half
¾ cup chicken broth
¼ cup ruby port
Salt and ground white pepper to taste
Chopped fresh or crumbled dried thyme or sage leaves to taste
Pork drippings

Fresh thyme or sage sprigs for garnish (optional)
Fresh cherries or cranberries for garnish (optional)

In a small bowl, mix together the olive oil and vinegar, and rub this mixture all over the pork roast. Sprinkle the roast evenly with salt, pepper, and thyme or sage, and rub the seasonings into the flesh. Let the pork roast sit at room temperature for 1 hour. If you are using dried cherries or cranberries, place them in a small bowl with the lemon juice and set aside.

Using extra coals, light a charcoal fire in a grill with a hood, dividing the coals between two charcoal baskets or charcoal rails, if you have them. When the coals are hot, if you are not using baskets or rails, divide the coals in half and push them to either side of the grill. Place a rectangular metal baking pan in the center of the fuel bed. Place the roast in the center of the grill over the drip pan and close the top vents slightly, leaving the bottom vents completely open.

Cover the grill and cook the roast for about 1 hour and 15 minutes, uncovering the grill every 15 minutes or so to check on the heat level of the fire; if the fire begins to die, shake or stir the coals and open the top vents completely. You also may want to add new coals to the fire; if so, light a charcoal chimney full of coals (be sure it is placed on a fireproof surface); when the coals are fully lighted, divide them between the two groups of coals already in the grill. The roast is done when an instant-read thermometer inserted into the thickest part reads 150°F.

About 20 minutes before the roast is due to be done, begin the sauce: In a medium saucepan, melt the butter and add the shallots; sauté until the shallots are translucent. Drain the dried cherries or cranberries, if using, reserving the juice, and add them to the pan. Stir in the half-and-half and cook over medium heat, stirring occasionally, for about 10 minutes, or until the liquid is slightly reduced. Stir in the chicken broth, port, and lemon juice and simmer over low heat for about 10 minutes. Add the fresh or frozen cherries or cranberries, if using and simmer for another 5 minutes. Add the salt, pepper, and herbs, and set aside.

When the roast is done, transfer it from the grill to a plate and cover it with aluminum foil; let sit for 10 minutes. Remove the foil and transfer the roast to a serving plate, reserving the drippings. Pour the drippings into the cherry sauce and heat until warm over low heat. Fill the cavity of the roast with wild rice and garnish the edges of the plate with more wild rice, herb sprigs, and cherries or cranberries, if you like. Carve the roast into ribs at the table and pass a sauceboat of the warm sauce.

Pork Loin Roast with a Cream Sauce of Port and Cherries: A 3- to 4-pound boneless rolled pork loin or pork sirloin roast will serve 6 to 8 people. Trim all but ¼ inch of fat from the roast, reserving it to grease the cooking rack. Use half the amount of oil, vinegar, and herbs to rub the roast. Using extra coals and a hot indirect fire, sear the roast on all sides for a total of 10 minutes. Cover the grill and cook the roast, fat-side up, for 15 minutes per pound, or until an instant-read thermometer inserted in the center reads 150°F. Make half the amount of sauce. Serve the roast cut into slices on a bed of wild rice, with the sauce poured over.

PORK KABOBS WITH APPLES, FENNEL, RED ONION, FIGS, AND SAGE VINAIGRETTE

Scalloped Sweet Potatoes · Radicchio Salad or Grilled Radicchio · Beaujolais

Serves 4

Savory pork combined with an interesting selection of fruits and vegetables is a fine grill meal for late summer or early fall. The fresh sage leaves add a special flavor note, and the sage vinaigrette is the perfect final touch for the kabobs. Serve with scalloped sweet potatoes and radicchio salad or grilled radicchio, and a fresh Beaujolais.

1½ pounds boneless pork shoulder or butt, trimmed of fat and cut into 1½-inch cubes
2 unpeeled apples, quartered, cored, and cut into eighths
1 fennel bulb, cut into 1-inch wedges
1 large red onion, peeled and cut into 1-inch wedges
12 whole fresh figs, or whole dried figs soaked in warm dry red wine to cover for 30 minutes
Fresh sage leaves (optional)

Marinade

2 tablespoons olive oil
2 tablespoons red wine vinegar
2 chopped garlic cloves
1 tablespoon chopped fresh sage, or 1 teaspoon crumbled dried sage leaves

Sage Vinaigrette

3 tablespoons chopped fresh sage, or 1 tablespoon crumbled dried sage leaves
½ cup olive oil
3 tablespoons white wine vinegar
Salt to taste

On long skewers, thread the pork cubes alternately with the apple, fennel, and red onion wedges, and the figs and sage leaves, if using. Place the kabobs flat in a shallow nonaluminum container. In a small bowl, mix together all the ingredients for the marinade and pour it over the kabobs. Marinate at room temperature for 30 minutes to 2 hours, or cover and marinate in the refrigerator for 2 to 4 hours; turn the skewers 2 or 3 times during this period. If the kabobs have been refrigerated, remove them from the refrigerator just before lighting the fire.

Light a charcoal fire in a grill with a hood. While the coals are heating, make the vinaigrette: In a small bowl, combine all the ingredients for the vinaigrette and set aside at room temperature.

When the coals are hot, sear the kabobs for 3 minutes on each side, turning them with long-handled tongs and basting them before turning the second time. Baste and turn the kabobs, cover the grill, and cook for 3 minutes on each side, basting before turning the second time, for a total cooking time of 12 minutes, or until the center of a kabob is barely pink.

Transfer the kabobs from the grill to a plate, cover them with aluminum foil, and let sit for 5 minutes. Serve with sage vinaigrette as a dipping sauce or a dressing for the kabobs.

HICKORY-SMOKED BABY BACK RIBS

Corn on the Cob with Lime Butter · Marinated Red Onion and Romaine Salad · Grilled Yam Slices · Imported Beer

Serves 4

Meatier and less fatty than spareribs, baby back ribs have become a favorite for the grill. A light marinade of beer and crushed red pepper and the woodsy taste of hickory smoke give these ribs a succulent flavor. It's easy to grill thin lengthwise slices of yams along with the ribs. We also like a salad of marinated red onions (page 54) and romaine, and corn on the cob with lime butter with this dish. Serve with your favorite imported beer.

6 pounds baby pork back ribs

Marinade

½ cup beer
1 tablespoon olive oil
1 tablespoon low-salt soy sauce
1 chopped yellow onion
½ to 1 teaspoon dried red pepper flakes
2 teaspoons honey

1 cup hickory chips
2 yams
Olive oil for brushing

Place the ribs in a large, shallow nonaluminum container. In a small bowl, mix together all the marinade ingredients and pour over the ribs. Marinate for 30 minutes to 2 hours at room temperature, or from 2 to 4 hours in the refrigerator, turning the ribs 3 or 4 times during this period. If the ribs have been refrigerated, remove them from the refrigerator just before lighting the fire.

Light a charcoal fire in a grill with a cover. Place the hickory chips in water to cover. Scrub the yams well and cut them into ½-inch-thick lengthwise slices. Brush them on both sides with olive oil.

When the fire is hot, drain the hickory chips well and sprinkle them evenly over the coals. Place the yam slices around the edges of the cooking rack. Place the ribs flesh-side down in the center of the cooking rack, cover the grill, and cook for 5 minutes. Baste and turn the ribs, cover the grill, and cook another 5 minutes. Baste and turn the ribs twice more, cooking them for 10 minutes on each side, for a total cooking time of 30 minutes, or until they are cooked to the depth of color you prefer; turn the yam slices as needed until they are well browned and tender. Transfer the ribs from the grill to a plate and let sit for 5 minutes before serving with the yam slices.

PORK SPARERIBS IN A HOT BEAN PASTE MARINADE

Apple, Red Onion, and Red Cabbage Coleslaw · Chinese Noodle Salad with Sesame Oil
Spicy German White Wine or Chinese Beer

Serves 4

A tasty recipe for ribs with the kick of pungent Chinese bean paste and citrus juice. We've used tangerine juice for its deep, sweet flavor, but you can substitute a mixture of orange and lemon juices. Serve these ribs with a coleslaw of red cabbage, red onions, and apples (with minced cilantro), and a Chinese noodle salad with sesame oil. To drink: a spicy German white wine or Chinese beer.

4 pounds pork spareribs

Marinade

2 tablespoons hot bean paste
¼ cup rice wine vinegar
1 tablespoon low-salt soy sauce
1 tablespoon dried tangerine peel, or
zest of 1 tangerine or orange, cut into fine strips
3 or 4 garlic cloves, crushed
2 tablespoons peanut oil
Juice of 4 large tangerines, or 2 oranges and 2 lemons

Slices of tangerine or orange for garnish
Fresh cilantro sprigs for garnish (optional)

Place the spareribs in a large, shallow nonaluminum container. In a medium bowl, mix together all the ingredients for the marinade and pour it over the ribs, turning them several times to coat them evenly. Cover and marinate in the refrigerator for 8 hours or overnight, turning the ribs several times during this period. If the ribs have been refrigerated, remove them from the refrigerator just before lighting the fire.

Light a charcoal fire in a grill with a hood. When the coals are hot, sear the ribs for 3 minutes on each side, basting them with the marinade before turning them the second time. Baste and turn the ribs again, cover the grill, and cook the ribs for 10 minutes. Baste and turn the ribs again, cover the grill, and cook the ribs for another 10 minutes (a total cooking time of 26 minutes), or until browned to your taste. Transfer the ribs from the grill to a platter and let sit for 5 minutes before serving. To serve, garnish with slices of tangerine or orange, and cilantro sprigs, if you like.

VINE-SMOKED RABBIT WITH
A SAUCE OF RED WINE AND FRESH HERBS

Mustard Greens Braised in Olive Oil and Chicken Broth · Pasta with Four Cheeses · Bruschette
Spanish Red Wine

Serves 3 to 4

Although rabbit meat is almost as delicate in flavor as chicken, it takes well to pungent marinades and sauces, like this rich reduced wine sauce with garlic and chopped fresh herbs. Add more herbs to the fire to give their fragrance to the winey scent of the grapevine cuttings. Serve this dish on a fine summer or autumn evening, with mustard greens braised in olive oil and chicken broth, pasta with four cheeses, and bruschette: grilled slices of country bread rubbed with garlic and drizzled with olive oil. Grilled polenta or a soft polenta blended with Parmesan cheese could substitute for the pasta. Try a good Spanish red wine with this menu.

1 rabbit, cut into 6 serving pieces

Marinade

2 cups dry red wine
½ cup olive oil
4 or 5 garlic cloves, chopped
2 tablespoons chopped mixed fresh herbs such as
   rosemary, thyme, sage, and oregano, or
   2 teaspoons mixed dried herbs

1 cup grapevine cuttings
Herb stems and sprigs for the fire (optional)

Red Wine and Herb Sauce

Reserved marinade, above
1 teaspoon flour
1 teaspoon butter
½ cup dry red wine
¼ cup canned low-salt beef broth, or more
Chopped fresh or dried herbs to taste
Salt to taste

Clusters of grapes and herb sprigs for garnish
   (optional)

Place the rabbit pieces in a large nonaluminum bowl. In a medium bowl, combine all the ingredients for the marinade and pour it over the rabbit, turning the pieces to coat them well. Cover and marinate for 4 to 8 hours or overnight in the refrigerator, turning the rabbit pieces 2 or 3 times during this period. If the rabbit has been refrigerated, remove it from the refrigerator just before lighting the fire.

Light a charcoal fire in a grill with a hood. Place the grapevine cuttings and any leftover herb stems and sprigs (save some sprigs for garnish) in water to cover.

When the coals are hot, sear the rabbit pieces on each side for a total of 5 minutes. Drain the herbs and grapevine cuttings well and sprinkle them evenly over the coals. Baste the rabbit with the marinade, turn the pieces over, cover the grill, partially close the upper vents, and cook for 15 minutes. Baste and turn the rabbit again, cover the grill, and cook the rabbit for another 15 minutes (a total cooking time of 35 minutes). Transfer the rabbit from the grill to a plate, cover it with aluminum foil, and let it sit while making the wine sauce.

To make the sauce: Pour all the remaining marinade into a small saucepan and cook over medium-high heat for 2 or 3 minutes, or until it is thick and glossy. Stir in the flour, then the butter, and cook for 2 to 3 minutes, stirring, until slightly thickened and smooth. Whisk in the wine and beef broth and cook for another 5 minutes to burn off the alcohol and reduce the liquid to a smooth sauce. Add the chopped fresh or dried herbs and salt to taste. Serve the rabbit on a pool of sauce and garnish with grapes and herb sprigs, if you like.

GRILLED VEAL CHOPS WITH FRESH OREGANO

Braised Fresh Fava Beans · *Chard Cooked in Olive Oil with Garlic and Pancetta, or Green Salad with Parmesan* · *Frascati*

Serves 4

One of our easiest recipes: thick veal chops marinated in olive oil and balsamic vinegar and sprinkled with chopped fresh oregano. Serve on a bed of braised fresh fava beans or other shelling beans (or cannelloni or other dried white beans), along with chard cooked in olive oil with garlic and pancetta. A green salad with shavings of aged Parmesan could substitute for the chard; to drink, try a chilled Frascati.

Four 1-inch-thick veal chops

Marinade

2 tablespoons olive oil
2 tablespoons balsamic vinegar
2 garlic cloves, chopped
2 tablespoons chopped fresh oregano, or
    2 teaspoons crumbled dried oregano

2 tablespoons chopped fresh oregano
    for sprinkling (optional)
Oregano sprigs for garnish (optional)

Trim the veal chops of any visible fat. Place them in one layer in shallow nonaluminum container. Mix together all the marinade ingredients and pour evenly over the chops. Marinate the chops for 30 minutes to 2 hours at room temperature, or cover and refrigerate for 2 to 4 hours, turning the chops 2 or 3 times during this period. If the chops have been refrigerated, remove them from the refrigerator just before lighting the coals.

Light a charcoal fire in a grill with a hood. When the fire is hot, grease the cooking rack with the reserved fat, using long-handled tongs, and sear the chops for 3 minutes on each side, basting with the marinade before turning the second time. Baste and turn the chops again, then cover and cook for 4 minutes on each side, basting before turning the second time (a total cooking time of 14 minutes).

Transfer the chops from the grill to a plate and sprinkle them evenly with 1 tablespoon of the chopped fresh oregano, if you like; turn and sprinkle the other side of the chops evenly with the remaining oregano. Let the chops sit for 5 minutes, then serve them on a bed of beans, garnished with oregano sprigs, if you like.

GRILLED VEAL ROLLS WITH FRESH TOMATO-BASIL SAUCE

Malfatti or Orzo Cooked in Broth · Arugula Salad · Chianti Classico

Serves 4

Stuffed veal rolls are transformed by the grill into elegant dinner fare—and they're quick and easy to make. The fresh sauce takes a matter of seconds to prepare and is the perfect complement to the crusty but tender veal. Serve this main course with malfatti—fresh pasta chopped into uneven bits and pieces—or orzo, cooked in broth, and an arugula salad. Chianti Classico is the perfect wine for this meal.

8 slices veal scaloppine, or 8 veal scallops or cutlets

Stuffing

8 ounces ground pork
8 ounces ground veal
Salt and ground white pepper to taste
2 tablespoons butter
1 yellow onion, chopped
¼ cup chopped fresh basil
3 tablespoons freshly shredded Parmesan
1 tablespoon tomato paste

Olive oil for brushing

Fresh Tomato-Basil Sauce

2 vine-ripened tomatoes, about 6 Roma tomatoes, or 1 basket cherry tomatoes
2 tablespoons olive oil
¼ cup chopped fresh basil
1 or 2 garlic cloves, minced
Salt to taste

Basil sprigs for garnish
Red and yellow baby Roma tomatoes for garnish (optional)

Light a charcoal fire in a grill with a hood. While the coals are heating, make the veal rolls: If you are using veal scallops or cutlets, pound them as thinly as possible by placing them on a cutting board and hitting them with the side of a heavy bottle (you can also use a mallet with a smooth pounding surface, but don't use one with a jagged surface intended to be used to tenderize meat). Set the meat aside.

In a medium bowl, stir the ground pork and veal together with salt and pepper to taste. In a sauté pan or skillet, melt the butter, add the onion, and cook and stir until the onion is translucent. Add the meat, cooking and stirring it just until it loses its color, about 4 minutes. Stir in the basil, Parmesan, and tomato paste; adjust the seasoning with salt and pepper.

Spread 2 tablespoons or so of the stuffing evenly over a piece of veal and roll the veal up, rather loosely, like a jelly roll; take care not to roll it tightly, otherwise the stuffing will be pressed out. Tie crosswise with cotton string in 3 or 4 places. Repeat to make 8 veal rolls. Brush all of the rolls with olive oil.

When the coals are hot, sear the veal rolls all over for a total of 2 minutes. Cover the grill and cook the rolls for 4 minutes, then turn, cover, and cook them for another 4 minutes (a total cooking time of 10 minutes), or until they are well browned on both sides.

Transfer the veal rolls to a plate and let sit while you make the sauce: Chop the tomatoes rather coarsely. Place them in a small bowl and stir in the remaining ingredients. Garnish the serving plate with basil and the baby Romas, if you have them. Serve the bowl of fresh sauce alongside.

GRILLED VEAL ROAST WITH SAGE-HAZELNUT BUTTER

Fresh Pasta with Wild Mushrooms · Sautéed Baby Green Beans · Soave or Fumé Blanc

Serves 8 to 10

A boneless veal roast makes a grill meal that is both simple and elegant. The delicate taste of the veal is complemented by a quickly made sage-hazelnut butter; for a lighter sauce, spoon a little Sage Vinaigrette, page 73, over each serving. Try sautéed baby green beans and fresh pasta with wild mushrooms as side dishes, and accompany with a Soave or a Fumé Blanc.

> One 3¾- to 4-pound boneless veal roast
> Olive oil for drizzling and brushing
> Salt and ground white pepper to taste
> Fat from veal roast or 2 to 3 slices of pancetta or drained blanched bacon★
> 8 to 10 fresh sage leaves
> 3 or 4 garlic cloves, cut into slivers

Sage-Hazelnut Butter

> ⅓ cup toasted hazelnuts (filberts),★★ minced
> ½ cup whipped unsalted butter at room temperature
> ¼ cup minced fresh sage
> Salt and ground white pepper to taste
>
> Fresh sage sprigs for garnish

If the veal roast has been tied and barded with fat, remove it, discarding the strings and reserving the fat. Trim any fat from the roast, leaving no more than a ¼-inch layer; reserve the fat. Lay the roast flat, then drizzle and rub the interior with olive oil. Salt and pepper lightly.

Cut any barding fat you may have into a long strip about 1 inch wide and lay it the length of the roast, or use slices of pancetta, blanched bacon, or pieces of reserved trimmed fat. Place the sage sprigs along the length of the roast. Sprinkle the garlic slivers evenly over the surface. Roll the roast into a cylinder and tie with cotton string at 1-inch intervals. Rub olive oil evenly over the outside of the roast and insert whole sage leaves randomly under the string. Salt and pepper lightly.

Light a charcoal fire in a grill with a hood. When the coals are hot, grease the cooking rack with a piece of reserved fat, if you have some, and sear the roast all over for a total of 10 minutes. Brush the roast with olive oil and turn it over. Sprinkle any leftover sage stems on the fire, cover the grill, and cook the roast for 20 minutes. Brush the roast with olive oil again, turn, cover the grill and cook for another 20 minutes, for a total cooking time of 50 minutes, or until an instant-read thermometer inserted in the center of the roast reads 150°F. Remove the roast to a carving board and cover with aluminum foil; let sit for 15 to 20 minutes.

Meanwhile, make the sage-hazelnut butter: In a medium bowl, stir together all the ingredients until well blended and set aside.

Remove the strings from the veal roast and cut the roast into ½-inch-thick slices. Place a spoonful of the flavored butter on each serving, garnish with sage leaves, and serve.

★**To blanch bacon strips:** Cook the bacon strips in boiling water to cover for 10 minutes, then drain, rinse in cold water, and drain on paper towels.

★★**To toast hazelnuts:** Place the hazelnuts in a jelly-roll pan and toast them in a preheated 350°F oven for 8 minutes. Let cool, then place the nuts in a clean dish towel. Rub the hazelnuts together inside the towel to remove their skins.

GRILLED LOIN OF VENISON WITH FRESH CRANBERRY-CHILI CHUTNEY

Mesclun Salad · Leek Gratin · Spoon Bread · Pinot Noir or Barolo

Serves 8 to 10

The loin of venison is an excellent choice for entertaining. This boneless cut has no waste, is very low in fat, comes from naturally raised animals, and is large enough to serve 8 to 10 people; smaller cuts also are available. Farm-raised venison, which is milder in taste than wild venison, is available at specialty butcher shops in larger cities (you may have to order it ahead of time), or you can have it delivered to your door within 24 hours by calling an 800 number (see Equipment and Food Sources). Venison has a deeply sweet, flavorful taste that is enhanced by the flavor of charcoal and by assertive foods such as our sweet-hot fresh chutney of cranberries, orange, and jalapeño. We like this dish served with a salad of the mixture of baby greens called mesclun, leek gratin, and spoon bread. A Pinot Noir or Barolo goes nicely with venison.

1 boneless venison strip loin (about 4 pounds)
1 cup dry red wine
2 tablespoons olive oil
6 garlic cloves
1 teaspoon freshly ground black pepper, or more
Salt to taste

Fresh Cranberry–Chili Chutney

1 navel orange
1 cup fresh or frozen cranberries
½ large white onion, coarsely chopped
⅓ cup distilled white vinegar
¼ cup packed fresh mint leaves
1 small unseeded jalapeño chili, coarsely chopped
3 or 4 tablespoons sugar
Salt to taste

Mint sprigs and whole cranberries for garnish (optional)

Cut the venison in half crosswise for easier handling; place it on a large, shallow nonaluminum platter. In a small bowl, mix together the wine, olive oil, garlic, pepper, and salt. Pour this mixture over the venison, turning the meat to coat it evenly. Marinate at room temperature for 2 hours, or cover and place in the refrigerator for 4 to 8 hours or overnight, turning it several times during this period. If the venison has been refrigerated, remove it from the refrigerator just before lighting the charcoal.

Light a charcoal fire in a grill with a hood. While the coals are heating, make the chutney (it needs to sit at room temperature for at least 30 minutes to develop its flavors): Scrub the orange with a small brush under running water. Halve the orange crosswise and cut one half into coarse pieces. Juice the other half of the orange. Place the orange juice, the chopped orange, and all the remaining ingredients except the sugar and salt in a blender or food processor. Puree to a smooth sauce. Transfer the mixture to a bowl and add sugar and salt to taste. Set aside at room temperature.

When the coals are hot, sear the venison on each side for 3 minutes. Baste with the marinade, turn, baste again, cover the grill, and cook for 7 minutes. Baste, turn, baste again, cover the grill, and cook for another 7 minutes (a total cooking time of 20 minutes for rare to medium rare), or until an instant-read thermometer inserted into the thickest part of the loin reads 140°F for rare or 150°F for medium rare.

Transfer the venison from the grill to a carving board, cover with aluminum foil, and let sit for 10 to 15 minutes. Cut the venison into slices and serve with some of the juices poured over it; serve the cranberry chutney alongside.

Equipment and Food Sources

Grills

CHAR-BROIL
W.C. Bradley Enterprises
P.O. Box 1240
Columbus, GA 31993
404-571-7000 (in Georgia),
or 800-241-8981
Charcoal and gas grills,
smokers.

CHARMGLOW
500 South Madison
Du Quoin, IL 62832
618-542-4781
Gas grills and smokers.

DUCANE
800 Dutch Square Boulevard
Columbia, SC 29210-7376
803-798-1600
Gas grills.

HASTY-BAKE
P.O. Box 471285
Tulsa, OK 74147-1285
800-4AN-OVEN
Charcoal console grills and
built-ins.

KAMADO
BSW, Inc.
4680 East Second Street
Benicia, CA 94510
707-745-8175
Ceramic grill-ovens in
several sizes.

KINGSFORD COMPANY
P.O. Box 24305
Oakland, CA 94623-9981
800-537-2823
Charcoal kettle grills with
shelves, rack, and ash catcher.

THERMOS
Route 75
Freeport, IL 61032
800-435-5194
A wide range of gas console
grills with accessories.

OUTDOOR COMPANY
(O.D.C.)
P.O. Box 6255
Evansville, IN 47719-0255
800-544-5362
Accessories and replacement
parts for gas grills.

WEBER
Weber-Stephen Products
Company
560 Hicks Road
Palatine, IL 60067-6971
708-705-8660 (in Illinois),
or 800-323-7598;
fax 708-705-7971
Charcoal and gas kettle grills
in several sizes and styles;
grill accessories.

Charcoal and Smoking Woods

CHARCOAL COMPANION
7955 Edgewater Drive
Oakland, CA 94621
510-632-2100 (in California),
or 800-521-0505;
fax 510-632-1986
A wide variety of smoking
woods.

CONNECTICUT CHARCOAL
COMPANY
Old Time Charcoal
P.O. Box 742
Westport, CT 06881
203-227-2101
Hardwood charcoal.

DESERT MESQUITE OF
ARIZONA
3458 East Illini Street
Phoenix, AZ 85040
602-437-3135
Mesquite smoking woods.

HUMPHREY CHARCOAL
CORPORATION
P.O. Box 440
Brookville, PA 15825
814-849-2302
Wholesale and regional only;
call for names of distributors
of hardwood lump charcoal
and hardwood charcoal
briquettes.

LAZZARI FUEL COMPANY
P.O. Box 34051
San Francisco, CA 94134
415-467-2970 (in California),
or 800-242-7265
Mesquite charcoal and
smoking woods.

LUHR JENSEN & SONS, INC.
P.O. Box 297
Hood River, OR 97031
503-386-3811(in Oregon), or
800-535-1711
Smoking woods.

Grilling Accessories

CHARCOAL COMPANION
7955 Edgewater Drive
Oakland, CA 94621
510-632-2100 (in California),
or 800-521-0505;
fax 510-632-1986
A wide variety of grill
accessories.

GRIFFO PRODUCTS
1400 North 30th Street
Quincy, IL 62301
217-222-0700
Grilling grids and grill
baskets.

WEBER
Weber-Stephen Products
Company
560 Hicks Road
Palatine, IL 60067-6971
708-705-8660 (in Illinois), or
800-446-1070; fax
708-705-7971
Accessories for kettle grills;
grilling tools.

Naturally Raised Meats

Naturally raised beef and
other meats are available in
many natural foods stores
around the country, or you
can ask your local butcher
about carrying naturally
raised meats from some of
the many wholesalers in the
United States. Below are
some companies that sell
naturally raised meats by
mail order or regional home
delivery.

BIBLIOGRAPHY

BRAE BEEF
P.O. Box 1561
Greenwich, CT 06836
203-869-0106
Mail order worldwide of
naturally raised beef.

DAKOTA LEAN MEATS
136 West Trip
Winner, SD 57580
800-727-5326
Mail order nationwide of
naturally raised beef.

D'ARTAGNAN
399–419 St. Paul Avenue
Jersey City, NJ 07306
800-327-8246
Buffalo, rabbit, whole baby
lambs, New Zealand and
domestic farm-raised
venison.

DURHAM-NIGHT BIRD
358 Shaw Road, No. A
South San Francisco, CA
94080
415-737-5873
Naturally raised beef and
free-range veal, buffalo,
rabbit, whole baby lambs,
New Zealand and domestic
farm-raised venison.

THE GAME EXCHANGE
(retail); Polarica Game USA
(wholesale)
P.O. Box 880204
San Francisco, CA
94188-0204
415-647-1300 (in California),
or 800-GAME-USA
New Zealand and European
farm-raised vension, rabbit.

ORGANIC FOODS
WAREHOUSE
4399A Henninger Court
Chantilly, VA 22021
Mail order nationwide of
naturally raised beef, lamb,
pork, and poultry; regional
home delivery.

RICHMOND FARMS
R.D. 1, P. O. Box 525
Oxford, NJ 07863
908-689-0709
No mail order; home delivery
in New Jersey, metropolitan
New York, and eastern
Pennsylvania.

SUMMERFIELD FARMS
H.C. 4, P.O. Box 195A
Brightwood, VA 22715
703-948-3100
Mail order nationwide of
naturally raised veal, lamb.
venison, and poultry.

WOLFE'S NECK FARM
10 Burnett Road
Freeport, ME 04032
207-865-4469
Mail order nationwide and
regional home delivery of
naturally raised beef.

Center for Science in the Public Interest, Americans for Safe
Food Project. "Guide to Retail and Mail Order Sources of
Beef Produced Without Growth Hormones." Washington,
D.C.: June 1989.

Consumer Reports, "Gas Barbecue Grills," July 1991.

Editors of Time-Life Books. Outdoor Cooking. Alexandria,
Va.: Time-Life Books, 1983.

Ellis, Merle. Cutting Up in the Kitchen. San Francisco:
Chronicle Books, 1975.

Kilham, Christopher S. The Bread and Circus Wholefood Bible.
Reading, Mass.: Addison-Wesley, 1991.

Pépin, Jacques. La Technique. New York: New York Times
Book Co., 1976.

United States Department of Agriculture, Food Safety and
Inspection Service. Food News for Consumers, vol. 8, no. 1
(Spring 1991).

———. Preventing Foodborne Illness: A Guide to Safe Food Handling. Home and Garden Bulletin No. 247 (September 1990).

Chicken on the Grill

List of Recipes
with Suggested Accompaniments

Grill-roasted Chicken with Corn Bread Stuffing
Braised Swiss Chard
Grilled Tomato Halves
Sauvignon Blanc

Tom's Asian-style Drumettes
Grilled Chicken Sausages with a
    Selection of Mustards
Bruschette
Grilled Baby Leeks or Green Onions
Grilled Marinated Shrimp in the Shell
Chicory Salad
Cold Beer or Gamay Beaujolais

Grilled Chicken Breasts with Whole-Grain Mustard Sauce
Fresh Asparagus
Bulgur Pilaf
Light Amber Beer or Chardonnay

Grilled Mediterranean Chicken
Grilled Potato Slices
Green Salad
Sliced Tomatoes with Balsamic Vinegar
Chianti Classico

Thai-style Grilled Poussins with Peanut Sauce
Sticky Rice
Grilled Green Onions
Thai Beer

Cajun-style Grilled Chicken
Braised Mustard Greens
Spoon Bread or Grilled Cornmeal Mush
Cold Beer

Grilled Breaded Chicken Thighs
Potato Salad
Grilled Corn with Butter and Lime Juice
Sauvignon Blanc or Iced Tea

Chicken Fajitas
Fresh Salsa
Guacamole
Grilled Whole Poblano Chilies Stuffed
    with Goat Cheese
Corn or Flour Tortillas
Mexican Beer or Margaritas

Hot Fourth-of-July Barbecued Chicken
Grilled Unpeeled Potato Wedges
Shredded Red and Green Cabbage in
    Vinaigrette
Light Amber Beer or Ale

Grilled Chicken Breasts in Yellow Curry with Fresh Nectarine Chutney
Basmati Rice Pilaf with Aniseeds
Sautéed Sugar Snap Peas
Riesling

Whole Grill-roasted Chicken Stuffed with Wild Rice and Shiitake Mushrooms
Grilled Whole Garlic Bulbs
Green Salad
Grilled Country Bread
Zinfandel

Grilled Quail with Leeks
Risotto or Grilled Polenta
Mesclun Salad
Nebbiolo

Twice-grilled Duck Breast in a Raspberry Vinegar Marinade
Grilled Sliced Turnips and Whole Baby
    Carrots
Arugula Salad with Extra-virgin
    Olive Oil
Bordeaux

Chinese Barbecued Chicken
Chinese Noodle Salad
Grilled Japanese Eggplant
Chinese Beer or Gewürztraminer

Grilled Caribbean Chicken
Grilled Parsnips or Plantains
Braised Mustard Greens
Fresh Mango Chutney
Jamaican Beer

Grilled Cornish Hens with Chili Butter and Grilled-Corn Salsa
Hot Flour Tortillas
Mexican Beer

Tandoori Chicken Kabobs
Basmati Rice Pilaf with Saffron
Fresh Cilantro Chutney
Garlic Nan
Beer

Grilled Pheasant with a Sauce of Shiitake Mushrooms, Cream, and Brandy
Soft Polenta with Parmesan Cheese
Steamed Broccoli with Lemon Juice
Pinot Noir

Grilled Boned Turkey Breast Stuffed with Emmenthaler Cheese and Prosciutto
Potato Pancakes
Watercress Salad with Orange Slices
Chardonnay

Vegetables on the Grill
List of Menus

Grilled Port-marinated Chicken with Prunes
Garlic Mashed Potatoes
Braised Spinach or Brussels Sprouts
White Burgundy

Grilled Chicken Breasts with Apricot, Raisin, and Marsala Sauce
Sautéed Green Beans
Couscous with Pistachio Nuts
Sauvignon Blanc or Hot Mint Tea

Hickory-smoked Whole Chicken with Kansas City Barbecue Sauce
Grilled Sweet Potatoes
Creamy Coleslaw
Corn Bread
Beer, Iced Tea, or Lemonade

Vine-smoked Chicken Breasts with Herbs and Mustard-Cream Sauce
Grilled Halved Red Potatoes
Grilled Red Onion Wedges and
    Grilled Sliced Zucchini with
    Balsamic Vinegar
Chardonnay

Mesquite-smoked Chicken Breasts with Grilled Poblano-Tomatillo Sauce
Black Bean Salad
Chilaquiles
Mexican Beer or Fresh Limeade

Smoked Sesame Chicken on a Bed of Bitter Greens
Grilled Fennel Slices
Grilled Beet Slices
Green Onion Pancakes
Moselle or Riesling

Polenta with Green Chili and Red Pepper
Spicy Black Beans and Corn
Grilled Red Onions

Coconut, Lime, and Ginger-marinated Vegetables
Silver Noodles with Basil

Roasted Acorn Squash with Wild Rice Salad

Sandwich Grill
Smoked Gouda and Roasted Peppers on
    Rosemary Bread
Blue Cheese on Nut Bread
Swiss with Red Onion and Whole-Grain
    Mustard on Rye
Feta and Fennel on Italian Bread

Skewered Vegetables with Cilantro Sauce
Avocado and Jack Cheese Quesadillas

Yams, Apples, and Leeks with Spicy Pecan Nut Butter
Whole Corn on the Cob

Fresh Figs and Vegetables with Couscous
Parsley-Mint Sauce

Baby Vegetables with Pasta and Fresh Herb Sauce

Root Vegetables with Warm Mustard Greens Sauce

Skewered Tofu, Mushrooms, Daikon, and Bok Choy with a Soy, Ginger, and Orange Marinade

Grilled Appetizers
Dry Jack Cheese in Grape Leaf Wrappers
Yam Rounds on Focaccia Squares
Skewered Artichoke Hearts and Cherry
    Tomatoes
Thin Asparagus with Creamy Lemon
    Vinaigrette
Grilled Apples and Pears

Corn Bread–stuffed Peppers with Chipotle Sauce
Mango Salsa

Middle Eastern Eggplant Sandwich with Tahini Dressing

Vegetable Medley with Three Dipping Sauces
Curry-Ginger Sauce
Poppyseed-Orange Vinaigrette
Aïoli with Basil
Three-Grain Rice

Summer Salad with Quinoa
Lemon-Mustard Vinaigrette

Corn Cakes with Roasted Vegetables
Orange Cream Sauce

Vegetables with Northern Indian Almond-Spice Sauce

Garlicky Portobello Mushrooms
Spaghetti with Piquant Green Sauce

Basil and Pine Nut Polenta
Salsa Cruda

Grilled Tempeh with Red Onion and Eggplant on Whole-Wheat Toast
Sweet Lemon Mayonnaise

Eggplant, New Potato, and Fennel with Sour Cream Sauce
Grilled Artichokes

Tofu Satay with Tangy Dipping Sauce

Grill Cocktail Party
Grilled Japanese Eggplant
Grilled Belgian Endive
Roasted Whole Heads of Garlic
Toasted Bread Slices

Wood-smoked Pizzas
Garlic and Mushroom Topping
Eggplant and Goat Cheese Topping
Fennel and Tomato Topping
Sun-dried Tomato and Olive Topping

The Art of Grilling
List of Menus

Grilled Italian Appetizers
Smoked Parmigiano with Assorted
 Breads
Bruschetta with Grilled Eggplant
Scallops Grilled with Basil and
 Prosciutto
Imported Olives
Grape and Fig Bowl
Dry Italian White Wine

Tandoori Chicken
Papadums
Grilled Broccoli with Yogurt-Cumin
 Sauce
Basmati Rice Pilaf with Mustard and
 Fennel Seeds
Raita and Chutneys
Lager

**Rack of Lamb with Port, Rosemary,
 and Garlic Marinade**
Grilled New Potatoes
Sautéed Sugar Snap Peas
Tender Greens Salad

**Soft-Shell Crab with Hazelnut
 Butter**
Grilled Skewered Leeks and Mushrooms
Ribboned Carrot Salad
Fumé Blanc

Burgers and Red Onion Slices
Salad of Grilled Potato and Fennel
Sliced Beefsteak Tomatoes
Poppyseed Kaiser Rolls
Red Wine

**Boneless Quail with Corn Bread
 and Escarole Stuffing**
Grilled Parsnips
Steamed Asparagus
White Wine

Peppers Stuffed with Eggplant
Grilled Skewered Summer Squash with
 Rosemary Oil
Sliced Fruit with Yogurt-Mint Dressing
White Wine

Prawns with Spicy Remoulade
Steamed Greens
Grilled Cornmeal Mush Slices
Chardonnay

**Tenderloin of Beef with Mustard-
 Mint Sauce**
Couscous with Sautéed Figs
Steamed Artichokes with Creamy
 Vinaigrette
Pinot Noir

**Calves' Liver with Sage Butter and
 Pancetta**
Tuscan White Beans with Grilled Red
 Onion
Romaine Lettuce Salad with Creamy
 Parmesan Dressing
Saltless Italian Bread
Pinot Noir

**Lime-marinated Rock Cornish
 Game Hens**
Baked Black Beans, Corn, and Green
 Chilies
Mixed Green Salad with Orange
 Vinaigrette
Warm Tortillas
Beer

Ham Steak with Apple Cream Sauce
Grilled Sweet Potatoes
Braised Escarole
Popovers
Rosé

**Grapevine-smoked Salmon, Trout,
 and Oysters**
Fresh and Dried Bean Salad with Chive
 Vinaigrette
Oven-roasted Asparagus
Assorted Breads and Herbed Cream
 Cheese
White Wine

**Veal Roast with Marsala and Dried
 Apricots**
Pasta with Grilled Mushrooms
Radicchio with Walnut Vinaigrette
Bread Sticks
Red Wine

**Hickory-grilled Pork Chops with
 Fresh Peaches**
Spicy Black-eyed Peas
Steamed Swiss Chard with Mustard
 Vinaigrette
Corn Sticks
White Wine

Rabbit with Pecan Butter and Apples
Steamed Brussels Sprouts
Gougère
White Wine

Monkfish with Caper Vinaigrette
Grilled Belgian Endive
Steamed Carrots with Cream
French Bread
White Wine

GRILL BOOK
List of Menus

Steak Teriyaki Rice Bowl
Grilled Japanese Eggplant
Spinach-Sesame Salad
Japanese Beer

Thai Barbecued Chicken
Snow Peas with Toasted Sesame
  Dressing
Silver Noodles with Cucumber, Carrot,
  and Rice Vinegar
Lager

Spiedini with Balsamic Marinade
Grilled Fennel
Pasta with Brandy-Basil Cream Sauce
Arugula and Red Leaf Lettuce Salad
Italian Red Wine

Swordfish with Pico de Gallo
Grilled Green Tomatoes
Corn on the Cob
Hard Sourdough Rolls
Beer

**Turkey Breast Smoked with Cherry
  Wood**
Three-Pepper Relish and Cranberry
  Chutney
Hearty Vegetable Salad with Herbed
  Aïoli
Custard Corn Bread

**Sea Bass on Bok Choy with Ginger-
  Garlic Butter**
Peanut-Sesame Noodles
Steamed Chinese Long Beans
White Wine

**Hickory-smoked Country-style Ribs
  with Barbecue Sauce**
Herbed Twice-baked Potatoes
Wilted Red Cabbage Salad
Beer

**Butterflied Leg of Lamb with
  Zinfandel Sauce**
Grilled Turnips
Braised Spinach with Toasted Almonds
Crusty Italian Bread

**Veal Chops with Gruyère and
  Prosciutto**
Grilled Polenta with Pesto
Grilled Pattypan Squash
Roasted Red Pepper Salad

**Skewered Scallops, Zucchini, and
  Artichoke Hearts with Salsa**
Herbed Rice
Cold Lemon Asparagus

Grilled Whole Trout
Grilled Mixed Vegetables with Aïoli
Arugula, Limestone, and Red Leaf
  Lettuce Salad with Avocado

Grilled Steak with Fresh Herbs
Grilled Sweet Corn
Caesar Salad
Sourdough Bread

Salmon Steaks with Chive Butter
Grilled Japanese Eggplant
Grilled Scallions
Cold Pasta Salad

**Tofu Marinated in Sesame Oil and
  Rice Vinegar with Scallions**
Grilled Whole Chilies
Sliced Fresh Fruit
Cold Soba Noodles

**Rock Cornish Game Hens in
  Raspberry Vinegar Marinade**
Grilled Pears
Grilled Mushrooms
Steamed Fresh Green Beans with Water
  Chestnuts

Sesame Flank Steak
Grilled Whole Potatoes
Sautéed Fresh Okra
Sliced Tomatoes with Olive Oil and
  Basil

**Boneless Pork Loin in Sherry
  Vinegar, Port, and Prune
  Marinade**
Grilled Carrots
Herbed Potatoes
Tossed Greens

Grilled Split Lobster Tail
Roasted Garlic Heads
Butter Lettuce and Watercress Salad
Baguette

Mixed Sausage Grill
Grilled Red Onion Quarters
Red Cabbage with Apples
Dark German Bread

Chicken Breasts in Many Mustards
Grilled Gravenstein Apple Slices
Grilled Baby Leeks
Radicchio Salad

Nam Prik Shrimp
Grilled Zucchini
Tomato Pasta with Olive Oil and Lemon
  Zest

**Grilled Breast of Duck in Red Wine
  Marinade**
Grilled Crookneck Squash
Wild Rice with Green Onions and
  Mushrooms
Belgian Endive Salad with Toasted Pine
  Nuts

Peanut Chicken on Skewers
Rice with Lemon Grass and Coconut
Carrot Salad with Green Papaya

**Barbecued Baby Back Pork Ribs in
  Honey, Tamari, and Orange
  Marinade**
Grilled Yam Slices
Waldorf Salad
Corn Muffins with Green Chilies

Grill Appetizer Party
Topinka
Grilled Oysters and Clams on the Shell

Index

A
aïoli, 58
alder-smoked brisket, 47
apple-sherry sauce, 66
apples with pork kabobs, 73
Asian sesame oil, 34

B
baby back ribs, hickory-smoked, 74
balsamic vinegar, 34
basil-tomato sauce, 83
basting brush, 21
bay leaves with lamb kabobs, 62
beef, 25–28
   brisket, alder-smoked, 47
   doneness of, 25
   flank steak, marinated, 44
   grades of, 25–26
   hamburger, variations on, 54
   Korean barbecued, 51
   New York steak with brandy and black pepper sauce, 39
   Porterhouse steak with a sauce of shallots and Jim Beam, 41
   satay with Japanese eggplant and peanut sauce, 49
   steak fajitas, 52
   tenderloin with horseradish and watercress sauces, 42
black pepper and brandy sauce, 39
briquettes, 16, 19
brisket, 27, 47
broth, 34
butter, sage-hazelnut, 85

C
carving board, 21
charcoal
   baskets, 18
   briquettes, 16, 19
   chimney, 17, 20
   hardwood, 16, 19
   lighting, 17
   mesquite, 16, 19
   preparing a bed of, 17, 18
   rails, 18, 21
   replenishing, 19
   starter, 17
   storing, 20
   water smoker 16
cherry, cream, and port sauce, 70
chili(es), 35
   cranberry chutney, 86
   paste, 47
chops
   cooking tips for, 25
   lamb, 28, 30
   pork, 30, 64
   veal, 31, 81
chutney
   chili-cranberry, 86
   cucumber, 61
citrus peels, 20
cleanliness guidelines for cooking meat, 31–33
club steak, 27, 39
compote, dried fruit, 69
cooking
   rack, 17, 20
   times, 19, 34
covered grilling, 18
cranberry (ies), 34, 70
   chili chutney, fresh, 86
   cream, port, and cherry sauce, 70
crown roast, 30, 70
cucumber chutney, 61
cutting board, 21

D
doneness
   judging, 19
   temperatures, 25

dried
   cherries and cranberries, 34, 70
   fruit compote, warm, 69
   tangerine peel, 34, 77
drip pans, 18–19, 21

E
eggplant, Japanese, 49
electric
   grills, 16
   starter, 17

F
fajitas, 28, 52
fennel with pork kabobs, 73
figs with pork kabobs, 73
filberts, 35
fillet, beef, 26
fire
   adding flavors to, 20
   extinguishing, 20
   flare-ups, 19
   fuels for, 14, 16
   heat levels of, 17–18
   preparing, 17
   regulating, 18
   replenishing, 19
   starting, 17
fish sauce, 34
flank steak, 28, 44
flare-ups, 19

G
garam masala, 61
garlic, 34
   yogurt sauce, 62
gas grills, 14–16
ginger, 34
   dipping sauce, 51
grapevine cuttings, 20, 78
grill(s), 13–16
   basket, 21
   brush, wire, 20
   charcoal-water smoker, 16

(continued)
   cleaning, 17, 20
   console, 13
   covered, 18
   electric, 16
   fire starters, 17
   fuels, 14, 16
   gas, 14–16
   kamado, 13
   kettle, 13
   mitts, 21
   rack, preparing, 17
   secrets of, 33–34
   shutting down, 20
   stove-top, 16
   thermometer, 21
   tools, 20–21
   vents, 18
grilling grid, 21
ground meats, 25, 27, 54, 83
guacamole, 54

H
ham, 31
hamburger(s), 25, 54
hardwood charcoal, 16, 19, 20
hazelnut(s), 35
   sage butter, 85
   to toast and peel, 85
herb(s), 20, 35; see also specific herbs
   and red wine sauce, 78
hickory-smoked baby back ribs, 74
hoisin sauce, 35
horseradish sauce, fresh, 42
hot bean paste, 35
   marinade, 77
hot chili paste, 35

I
indirect grilling, 16, 18
instant-read thermometer, 20

J
jalapeño chilies, 35
Jim Beam and shallots

(continued)
sauce, 41

K
kabobs, 27, 28, 30, 31, 62, 73; see also satay
kamado, 13
Kansas City strip steak, 27, 39
kettle grill, 13
kidneys, lamb, 31
Korean barbecued beef, 51

L
lamb, 28–30
   doneness of, 25
   kabobs with summer vegetables and bay leaves, 62
   kidneys, 31
   leg of, butterflied, with Indian spices, 61
   rack of, marinated in pomegranate juice, 56
   saddle of, olive wood–smoked, 58
   sweetbreads, 31
leeks, grilled, 51
liver, calves', 31

M
marinade, 33, 35
   containers, 21
   hot bean paste, 77
meats, 25–31; see also specific kinds
   cooking safely, 30–31
   cutting up, 33
   doneness of, 25, 33
   guide to grilling, 33–34
   marinating, 33
   naturally raised, 25
   preparing for grill, 19, 33
   refrigerating, 33
   resting after grilling, 34